The Great Depression

An Enthralling Guide to the Worst Economic Downturn in the History of the Industrialized World

Free limited time bonus

We forget 90% of everything that we've read in 7 days...

Get the free printable pdf summary of the book you've read AND much, much more... shhhh...

Enter Your Most Frequently Used Email to Get Started

DOWNLOAD FREE PDF SUMMARY

© Enthralling History

Stop for a moment. We have a free bonus set up for you. The problem is this: we forget 90% of everything that we read after 7 days. Crazy fact, right? Here's the solution: we've created a printable, 1-page pdf summary for this book that you're reading now. All you have to do to get your free pdf summary is to go to the following website: **https://livetolearn.lpages.co/enthrallinghistory/**

Or, Scan the QR code!

Once you do, it will be intuitive. Enjoy, and thank you!

Table of Contents

Introduction

There are days in the story of humankind that are bleak reminders of our ability to rise to the occasion and defeat challenges. The Great Depression, which was a time of anxiety and worry, was one of those days. It was a period in history when the world faced unprecedented economic trouble, social unrest, and danger. Yet, despite frightening obstructions, great courage and a spirit of innovation emerged that turned the course of the 20th century. This book examines those unstable days. It is a tale of the defeats and triumphs of individuals, families, and nations. It tells the story of human strength in the face of ominous trials and of hope despite the depths of despair.

The Great Depression changed people, society, politics, and culture. Issues of income inequality, homelessness, and unemployment became highly visible features of the American landscape. Public officials and policymakers were confronted with the consequences of poor policies and forced to address them. The bonds of families and the resilience of communities were strained to the limit. The Great Depression demanded that Americans reconsider their traditions, dreams, and ambitions.

Discover the causes and consequences of the Great Depression. Examine the economy, market behaviors, societal undercurrents, and government actions that led to the ultimate tragedy. We will walk along the grim lanes of the Hoovervilles, stand in breadlines and soup kitchens with the unemployed, and watch as families roam the country with the belongings they could carry.

We will investigate the government response, particularly Franklin D. Roosevelt's New Deal, and its impact on the nation's recovery. The arts, literature, and culture of the 1930s allowed artists and writers to capture the essence of the human experience. Marginalized communities were faced with grave problems but contributed to the final recovery in spite of the difficulties. We will explore how they did that.

This book does more than quote facts and figures. Our present society was shaped by the events of that momentous era. We can still feel the influence it has on government policy and our understanding of determination and strength of character in the face of staggering adversity.

The Great Depression is no distant tale of bygone days. It is an essential part of the story of who Americans are and how the global community responds to a crisis. It is a tribute to our ability to face hopelessness and emerge stronger, wiser, and more compassionate.

It was a dark period, but there were flickers of light. Extraordinary people found the strength to rise from the ashes and could be found in all walks of life in those days. Their experiences are a testament to the indomitable human spirit and a reminder that, even in the worst of times, there is the potential for a brighter tomorrow.

Chapter 1: Before the Depression, the Wall Street Boom

A Roaring Mirage

What made the Great Depression so terrible was the period of positivism that came before the fall. The Roaring Twenties was a time of uplifting moods in the United States. World War I had ended, and the boys came home to an economy in high gear due to wartime production. Women finally had the right to vote, and society was moving forward confidently. Prosperity was in the air. Middle-class families were experiencing levels of wealth they never knew before, thanks to rising wages. Consumers could splurge on automobiles, clothes, and radios. These products were not very expensive, so they were affordable to the common person. For instance, Henry Ford's introduction of the assembly line to the automobile industry made purchasing a car at affordable prices easy. People moved from the country into urban areas and enjoyed the fast pace of city living. It all seemed to be the best of times for American society. At least, that was what it appeared to be.[1]

---

[1] Deceptology. (2022, November 29). The Prosperity of the 1920s: An Illusion for Many. Retrieved from Deceptology.com: https://www.deceptology.com/deceptive/the-prosperity-of-the-1920s-an-illusion-for-many.html.

Economic Productivity

Figures showed there was a degree of truth to the idea that the United States was experiencing an economic boom. A brief recession occurred at the start of the decade, but the gross national product (GNP) began to rise significantly in 1922, and it continued to rise higher and higher. The real GNP in 1920 was $677.7 billion, reaching $977 billion by 1929.

The golden child of the economy was the stock market. The Dow Jones Industrial Market went from 63.9 points in August 1921 to 381 points before Black Friday in October 1929, a jump of over 500 percent.

How stocks were purchased was a principal reason for the dramatic increase. Consumers were allowed to buy shares with margin calls. A margin call is a form of loan on Wall Street. An investor was required to come up with 10 to 20 percent of a stock's price, and the stockbroker buying the shares would loan the investor the remaining amount. A person could buy more shares and make sizable profits if the stock price increased.

Margin calls were a seductive, get-rich-quick financial instrument. A seasoned market professional could manage any swing in the stock prices. An amateur, however, would be in trouble if the stock price suddenly went down. That person still owed what was lent to them, and a price collapse could result in a severe debt situation for the unlucky rookie.[2]

The Banks

The American economy experienced boom and bust cycles in the stock market but was able to recover and move forward. There was more to the Roaring Twenties mirage than ticker tape. The banking system in the United States was dangerously vulnerable. Let's look at some key factors as to why that was the case.

• Lack of Sufficient Federal Oversight

In the 1920s, the United States did not have a centralized national agency that was able to regulate the banking sector and comprehensively oversee fiscal activity. Individual states regulated banking within their borders, resulting in a fragmented and inconsistent regulatory landscape. State regulation might include requirements that demand banks be local

---

[2] Amadeo, K. (2022, March 28). 1920s Economy. Retrieved from The balancemoney.com: https://www.thebalancemoney.com/roaring-twenties-4060511.

and have few branches, exposing the institutions to the consequences of a local economic downturn and regional bank failures.

The absence of a federal regulator allowed for variations in banking practices and standards across states, making it challenging to ensure systemic stability. State-chartered banks were not subject to consistent regulations, leading to significant variations in reserve requirements, capital adequacy, and lending practices.[3]

• Feeding the Beast

Banks at the time were guilty of aggressive lending practices and offered credit to individuals and businesses without sufficient collateral or serious risk assessment. A credit boom emerged, and start-up enterprises could borrow to support expansion, causing inventories to grow nearly out of control.

The banks played a significant role in generating the stock market surge. Margin buying in the stock market allowed investors to leverage their investments and permitted an unsustainable stock market bubble to expand. Banks loaned money to stock market speculators, and those investors used the cash to fund more margin calls.[4]

• Lack of Sufficient Safeguards

The Federal Reserve was not able to slow down the stampede into the Great Depression despite its attempts to warn banks of approaching storm clouds.

The value of the US dollar was tied to a fixed amount of gold. This constraint limited the ability to increase the money supply because the Federal Reserve had to maintain a specific gold reserve. This adherence to the gold standard would contribute to the Fed's inability to effectively stimulate the economy to end the financial crisis when it came.

During the 1920s, macroeconomics as a field of study was still in its early stages, and the Federal Reserve had a limited understanding of how the economy functioned on a broad scale. Policymakers followed ideas governed by classical economic thinking and firmly believed economic

---

[3] Firey, T. A. (2014, September 23). How Government Caused the Great Depression. Retrieved from The Maryland Public Policy Institute: https://www.mdpolicy.org/research/detail/how-government-caused-the-great-depression.

[4] McGee, S. (2021, May 13). How Bank Failures Contributed to the Great Depression. Retrieved from History.com: https://www.history.com/news/bank-failures-great-depression-1929-crash.

downturns would eventually correct themselves and did not require major government interventions. Consequently, significant public policy action was not deemed necessary.

Finally, banks ignored any warnings. It is estimated that more than 90 percent of all American banks had investments in the stock market. They were making too much profit with lending and stock market speculation to care. Tomorrow would take care of itself. Moreover, many banks were not part of the Federal Reserve system. These financial institutions made things potentially worse by having insufficient reserves. Unfortunately, the Federal Reserve did not make things any better by lowering the cash reserve limits banks were required to hold.[5]

Inadequate regulation and risky investment practices contributed to the severity of the economic downturn. These liabilities contributed to a collapse of confidence in the banking sector, forcing a chain reaction of economic chaos. The lessons learned from these weaknesses continue to inform banking regulation and the management of financial crises in the modern era, underscoring the enduring relevance of the historical analysis of the Great Depression.

The Real Economic Picture

Fantasy is always more entertaining than reality and blinds people to the warning signs of impending disaster. Everything looked wonderful on Wall Street, but matters were much different in the American heartland.

Considerable attention is given to the stock markets and the banks. Still, there were other signs, though not always direct harbingers of doom, that suggested the economy was heading into stormy waters.

• Overuse of Consumer Credit

It was often referred to as buying on time, and the public was increasingly turning to consumer credit as a means of buying. This was before the use of credit cards and installment sales agreements.

Installment buying was the principle means for consumers to buy now and pay later. It allowed people to purchase expensive items, such as radios, automobiles, and household appliances, on credit, paying for

[5] Florida State College at Jacksonville. (2023, December 23). The Great Depression and President Hoover's Response. Retrieved from fscj.pressbooks.pub:
https://fscj.pressbooks.pub/modernushistory/chapter/brother-can-you-spare-a-dime-the-great-depression/.

them in small, manageable monthly installments. The availability of installment credit made these consumer goods more accessible to a broader range of people, contributing to increased consumption and creating substantial economic growth during the decade.

However, there were a few caveats. Installment credit was primarily provided by retailers and manufacturers. The seller's discretion often determined creditworthiness. What developed was a problem that we hear about in modern society. A person's reliance on credit generated a surge in debt and a decline in savings.

Approximately 75 percent of the buying population spent most of their income buying things they did not always need. Outstanding consumer credit grew until it was more than $3 billion in 1929. Many households held substantial debt when Black Friday arrived.[6]

The Florida Land Boom

The Florida land boom was a speculative real estate frenzy that occurred in the state of Florida, particularly in the southern regions, during the early and mid-1920s. It did not cause the Great Depression, but it became one of the most iconic examples of a speculative bubble during the Roaring Twenties. It involved a rapid increase in land prices driven by a combination of factors.

- Real Estate Speculation: Speculators, investors, and individuals rushed to purchase land in Florida, especially in areas like Miami. Many believed that the state's climate and potential for development made it a prime location for real estate investment.

- Promotion and Marketing: Land developers and real estate agents engaged in aggressive marketing campaigns to lure buyers. They often used extravagant claims and exaggerated the potential for profits from land investments.

- Land Boom Cities: Cities in Florida experienced rapid population growth fueled by an influx of people attracted by the booming real estate market. New hotels, resorts, and infrastructure were built to accommodate the growing

[6] Angola Transparency. (2023, December 23). What Role Did Credit Play in the 1920s. Retrieved from Angolatrasparemcy.blog: https://angolatransparency.blog/en/what-role-did-credit-play-in-the-1920s/.

population and number of tourists.

- Rising Land Prices: Land prices in Florida soared to unsustainable levels. This speculative enthusiasm led to a bubble in land values.
- Financial Speculation: Just as with the stock market, many investors purchased land with credit, using borrowed money to finance their acquisitions. This leverage magnified the impact of the eventual crash.

The Florida land boom eventually peaked around 1925 and began to decline. The rapid construction of hotels, resorts, and other infrastructure outpaced demand and created a sizable inventory of unsold property, which caused property values to go down. As land prices began to fall, confidence in the market waned, leading to panic selling and land values collapsing.[7]

The Florida land boom of the 1920s is a textbook example of the speculative excess common in the 1920s American economy. There were some similarities between the Florida land boom and the broader economic conditions that led to the Great Depression:

- Speculative Mania: Both the Florida land boom and the stock market boom of the 1920s were characterized by speculative mania, where investors bought assets with the expectation of quick and substantial profits.
- Fragile Financial System: The excessive use of credit and margin buying in both real estate and stock markets made the financial system vulnerable to shocks.
- Economic Vulnerabilities: The 1920s saw income inequality, overproduction in agriculture, and other warning signs, as mentioned in a previous response, that contributed to the economic downturn.

Trouble Down on the Farm

The agricultural sector faced a severe downturn that foreshadowed the hardships of the Great Depression.

A major problem was overproduction. During World War I, American farmers increased their output to meet the wartime demand.

---

[7] Colombo, J. (2012, June 26). The 1920s Florida Real Estate Bubble. Retrieved from hebubblebubble.com: https://www.thebubblebubble.com/florida-property-bubble/.

Technological advancements in agriculture increased crop yields, but the innovations contributed to overproduction. Demand for agricultural products dramatically dropped after the war ended. The surpluses depressed crop prices and reduced farm income.

Many farmers took on large debts to finance expansion and equipment purchases during and after World War I. It was challenging to fund those loans when crop prices kept falling. The gross cash income for farmers dropped substantially. In Minnesota, gross cash income for farmers fell from $438 million in 1918 to $229 million in 1922. High debt and low income led to widespread financial hardship in farming counties. Sixty out of every one thousand farmers were forced into bankruptcy or lost their homesteads. Between 1922 and 1932, almost three thousand farmers in Minnesota declared bankruptcy.[8]

Diversification could have helped ease the plight, but the American agricultural sector relied heavily on a few staple crops, such as cotton and wheat, which meant farmers were susceptible to any fluctuation in the price of a single commodity. The fall in prices of agricultural commodities continued throughout the 1920s. Farmers were unable to recover their production costs, forcing many into desperate situations.

Droughts and tariff legislation added to the troubles American farmers were forced to manage. As farm income declined, rural communities suffered economic hardship. Small towns and rural areas experienced depopulation, as people moved to urban areas in search of better economic opportunities. The federal government's agricultural policies in the 1920s did not effectively address the challenges facing farmers. The McNary-Haugen Farm Relief Bill aimed to stabilize farm prices by raising the domestic price of several crops, but it faced political opposition and was never fully implemented.

In 1919, William Butler Yeats wrote his poem *The Second Coming*. It is an apocalyptical work that the poet uses to communicate his views of the chaos following World War I. It ends with these lines:

"And what rough beast, its hour come round at last,

Slouches towards Bethlehem to be born?"[9]

---

[8] Cameron, L. A. (2022, June 30). Agricultural Depression 1920-1924. Retrieved from Mnopedia.org: https://www.mnopedia.org/agricultural-depression-1920-1934.

[9] Yeats, W. B. (2923, December 23). The Second Coming. Retrieved from Poetry Foundation.org: https://www.poetryfoundation.org/poems/43290/the-second-coming.

It is a fitting commentary on the final days of the Roaring Twenties. There were all types of warning signals in the economy and in society that were not receiving adequate attention. Government policies and the mood of the buying public did not take into account the possibility that the good times were going to end and be followed by a horrific correction in the economy. Everything seemed to be just fine on the surface. Speculation, overuse of credit, and troubles on the farm created a terrifying scenario that would burst into American society in the last year of the 1920s. The worst of times was about to happen.

Chapter 2: The Wall Street Crash of 1929

Amid the bustling, jazz-filled streets of 1920s America, a seemingly unstoppable economic force was at play. The nation was riding high on a wave of prosperity fueled by industrialization, technological advancements, and a newfound sense of consumer optimism. The Roaring Twenties were a time of unprecedented economic growth, conspicuous consumption, and an unflinching public conviction that the future was going to be even better.

New York City epitomized the spirit of the times. George Gershwin's "Rhapsody in Blue," composed in 1924, captured the fast pace of urban life and the busy lifestyles of modern America. New York had become the premier symbol of the bustling times. Wall Street was in the heart of the Financial District and a symbol of American economic prowess. Wall Street was where the stock market was located, a place where paper fortunes were being made almost overnight. Stock prices climbed to breathtaking heights, and investors clamored to get in on the action. Individual investors bought on margin and hoped the loaned money would increase their wealth. The stock market seemed like a large fountain spewing money, and everything looked swell. Yet, beneath the glitz and glamor lay the beginnings of one of American history's most devastating financial disasters: the Wall Street crash of 1929.

The fall happened in a matter of a few days. The stock market plummeted, and panic spread like wildfire among investors. The repercussions of this crash were felt not only on Wall Street but also in households across the nation, marking the beginning of a dark chapter in American history.

The Start of the Fall

The year 1929 started on an upbeat note. A new president, Herbert H. Hoover, was sworn into office on March 4th, 1929. His inaugural address was positive, mentioning that America was a land "rich in resources, stimulating in its glorious beauty; filled with millions of happy homes; blessed with comfort and opportunity."[10]

Trouble Was Brewing

The optimistic inaugural address uplifted spirits, but there were economic issues that were starting to become significant problems. Supposedly good news was hiding the bad. In the months leading up to the Wall Street Crash on October 29th, 1929, there were warning signs and underlying factors in the stock market that suggested dramatic changes were on the horizon.

Speculation, encouraged by margin purchases, was driving stock prices higher. Those figures were not consistent with corporate earnings and assets. Securities were becoming dangerously overvalued, which indicated that a correction was coming; it was anybody's guess as to how large that would be. There were three particularly ominous signs, some of which were talked about in the previous chapter:

- Overvaluation: Stock prices had been on a prolonged upward trajectory. By the summer of 1929, many stocks were trading at significantly inflated prices compared to their actual earnings and assets. This overvaluation indicated that a correction was overdue. In the days leading up to the crash, there were increased signs of market volatility and large fluctuations in stock prices, which heightened investor anxiety.
- Reckless Consumer Investment: Playing the stock market was nearly out of control, and money that ought to have gone to commerce and industry was funding margin call loans. Some banks were heavily invested in the stock market, and their

---

[10] Gilderlehrman.org. (2023, December 23). Herbert Hoover's Inaugural Address, 1929. Retrieved from Gilderlehrman.org: https://www.gilderlehrman.org/history-resources/spotlight-primary-source/herbert-hoovers-inaugural-address-1929.

exposure to stock market losses raised concerns about the banking system's stability. Many Americans had accumulated high levels of debt due to the widespread use of installment buying for consumer goods. Rising consumer debt levels meant that people had less disposable income to invest in the stock market.[11]

- Declining Industrial Production: Manufacturing activity had started to decline in the months leading up to the crash. Automobile production, the jewel in the crown of the American economy, dipped from 660,000 units in March to 319,000 in October. These were indicators that the real economy was not as strong as stock prices suggested, and it raised concerns about corporate profits.[12]

Everything seemed headed for a major calamity.

The Warnings Were Ignored

Some economists and financial analysts cautioned that the stock market was overvalued and was due for a correction. They pointed to the disparity between stock prices and actual corporate earnings and asset values. Economist Rober Babson believed stock prices were significantly inflated compared to predictions of future dividends. His warning given to the National Business Conference in September 1929 was prescient:

"Sooner or later a crash is coming which will take in the leading stocks and cause a decline from 60 to 80 points in the Dow-Jones barometer. Someday the time is coming when the market will begin to slide off, sellers will exceed buyers and paper profits will begin to disappear. Then there will immediately be a stampede to save what paper profits then exist."[13]

---

[11] Richardson, G. (2013, September). Banking Crisis and the Federal Reserve as a Lender of Last Resort during the Great Depression? Retrieved from National Bureau of Economic Research: https://www.nber.org/reporter/2013number3/banking-crises-and-federal-reserve-lender-last-resort-during-great-depression.

[12] Au, T. (2015, January 21). Was the Stock Market Crash of 1929 a Cause or Result of the Great Depression? Retrieved from History.stackexchange.com: https://history.stackexchange.com/questions/19038/was-the-stock-market-crash-of-1929-a-cause-or-result-of-the-great-depression.

[13] Roos, D. (2023, March 27). Here Are Warning Signs Investors Missed before the 1929 Crash.

Like Cassandra from Greek mythology, Babson was ignored. Other warnings were often overlooked or dismissed.

Many investors were caught up in the speculative frenzy and believed the market would continue to rise. This "irrational exuberance" led many investors to believe that stock prices could only go higher. The fear of missing out on potential gains contributed to a herd mentality, where investors followed the crowd and ignored all the warnings of financial disaster. Looking back, it is clear that the warnings were prophetic, and there were indeed fundamental problems in the economy and the stock market. However, the combination of optimism, the belief in perpetual growth, limited regulation, and the herd mentality among investors led many to ignore or downplay the warnings. This contributed to the subsequent severity of the Wall Street Crash and the Great Depression that followed.

Herbert Hoover's inaugural address reflected the public's naïve confidence. "I have no fears for the future of our country. It is bright with hope."[14] That was said in March. Events in October dramatically changed things.

The Black Days

It took only six days in October to turn the financial world upside down. Panic selling triggered sharp drops in stock prices on October 24th, 1929. The culmination of events that came on Black Tuesday (October 29th, 1929) would lead to a catastrophic crash that generated significant financial losses and, in turn, created the Great Depression.

The days leading up to Black Tuesday, the infamous stock market crash of 1929, were marked by increasing volatility, investor anxiety, and a significant decline in stock prices.

October 24th, 1929—Black Thursday

October 24th, 1929, Black Thursday, was the beginning of the stock market crash of 1929. The Dow Jones Industrial Average (DJIA) dropped by 11 percent on that day. The collapse resulted from factors such as complications in the agricultural sector, an increase in interest rates, and a drop in consumer spending. Investor confidence was already

---

Retrieved from History.com: https://www.history.com/news/1929-stock-market-crash-warning-signs.

[14] Gilderlehrman.org. (2023, December 23). Herbert Hoover's Inaugural Address, 1929.

---

shaken, and the trading floor of the New York Stock Exchange (NYSE) was chaotic, with a flurry of sell orders. Trading volume was heavy, with 12.9 million shares of stock being traded.[15]

The Role of Margin Calls

Margin calls played a significant role in the day's turmoil.

Understanding margin calls is crucial to comprehending what happened. Stock prices were dropping sharply during the day, and many investors found themselves in a precarious position. As the stock values declined, the equity in their margin accounts shrank. When the equity in a margin account fell below the maintenance margin level, brokers issued margin calls to their clients. Those calls required that investors deposit additional funds or sell a portion of their holdings to cover the deficit.

Investors who received margin calls were faced with either depositing more money or selling their stocks to meet the call's demands. With widespread uncertainty and declining prices, many investors opted to sell. It caused further declines in stock value, especially since investors were increasingly receiving margin calls from their brokers. The effect of the margin calls is magnified when one understands that by the summer of 1929, approximately three hundred million shares were purchased on margin. Panic selling began to seize the market.[16]

As stock prices fell, some investors faced substantial losses that exceeded the value of their margin accounts. It meant that even after selling their stocks to meet the margin calls, they were still left with debts owed to their brokers and were forced to sell even more shares. The massive volume of selling overwhelmed the market, and the chain reaction of forced selling contributed significantly to the severity of the stock market crash.

While the day ended with a brief rebound, the market was in trouble, and investors were deeply concerned about their investments. Commercial banks intervened as the day progressed and bought stocks to restore investor confidence. The market closed down at 2 percent,

[15] History.com. (2023, November 16). Stock Market Crash of 1929. Retrieved from History.com: https://www.history.com/topics/great-depression/1929-stock-market-crash.

[16] Amadeo, K. (2021, January 27). Black Thursday 1929, What Happened, and What Caused It. Retrieved from The balance: https://www.thebalancemoney.com/black-thursday-1929-what-happened-and-what-caused-it-3305817.

which was a sizable drop but one that could be absorbed. It was possible that things might return to normal in the coming days.[17]

October 25th, 1929—Black Friday

There was a degree of optimism as the sun rose on Wall Street. Friday was another day of selling, but it opened with a small rally. Unfortunately, there was still selling pressure on the floor of the exchange, and the DJIA dropped 6.3 percent. The trading volume was 9.2 million shares. Some expressed hope that the problems were only temporary, but there was a heightened fear that more financial damage was yet to come.

The financial world breathed a sigh of relief when the closing bell finally rang on Friday, and the panicked trading stopped. The stock market was now closed for the weekend. Investors would have forty-eight hours to mull over what happened in the previous two days. They would decide what they would do with their money when the markets opened again.

Financiers and bankers were concerned about the direction the market was going and planned how to stabilize the market that weekend. There were behind-the-scenes discussions and negotiations. The men with money attempted to restore confidence in the system and prevent a total market collapse. They were not the only ones who were making plans for the upcoming days.

The Short Sale

Buying on margin was (and still is) not the only Wall Street tool for making money. There is another technique known as a short sale, and this financial strategy played a significant role the following week after Black Thursday.

Short sales are a means by which an investor takes advantage of a bear market. The investor will borrow shares from a broker and sell those securities on the open market, expecting the stock price to decrease in the near future. Once the price drops, the short seller then repurchases the stocks at the lower price and makes a profit, which is the difference between the original sales price and the lower repurchase price.

To illustrate what that means, suppose an investor believes that the price of Company A's stock will decline. The investor borrows one

---

[17] Amadeo, K. (2021, January 27). Black Thursday 1929, What Happened, and What Caused It.

hundred shares of Company A from a broker and sells the stock immediately for $50 a share, realizing $5,000 from the transaction. The investor then waits for the stock price to fall. Suppose, then, the stock of Company A drops to $40 a share. The investor then buys one hundred shares at the lower price, spending $4,000. The investor returns the shares they borrowed to the broker. The difference between the original $5,000 is realized from selling the stock, and then the repurchase amount of $4,000 is the profit the investor derives minus fees. The size of that profit rests with the drop in the share price.

The market activity of Black Thursday and Black Friday exposed an enormous opportunity for people who were willing to take the risk of short sales. It was in their best interests for the market to take another tumble.

October 28th, 1929—Black Monday

Monday was a day of reckoning for many investors. There were margin calls, but what really added to the problem was the short sales activity. General panic was prevalent on the trading floor. Any effort to try to push stock prices back up did not succeed. The DJIA dropped almost 13 percent in heavy trading. Psychology plays a role in financial speculation, and the mood of the investors in 1929 was one of sheer panic. The market was falling, and people hurried to find a way to cut their losses. There were all the ingredients for a selling frenzy that was not going to go away anytime soon. Wall Street was doomed.[18]

October 29th, 1929—Armageddon Day

Black Tuesday, October 29th, 1929, is one of the most infamous days in financial history and is often cited as the day the Wall Street Crash of 1929 reached its catastrophic climax. On this day, the stock market experienced a devastating collapse that marked the beginning of the Great Depression.

When the stock market opened on Black Tuesday, there was already great apprehension among investors. Selling pressure immediately intensified when investors rushed to sell their stocks. A massive wave of selling engulfed the market. Investors, both large and small, sought to liquidate their holdings to avoid further losses. The volume of trading

---

[18] Kenton, W. (2023, March 16). Stock Market Crash of 1929: Definition, Causes, Effects. Retrieved from Investopedia.com: https://www.investopedia.com/terms/s/stock-market-crash-1929.asp.

was unprecedented, with an astounding sixteen million shares changing hands during the day. Stock tickers ran behind because the machines were not able to handle the volume of trading. The financial losses were staggering. Fortunes were lost, and thousands of investors were financially destroyed. Delays created by the chaos only added to the problem.[19]

Stock prices plummeted at an alarming rate as margin calls and short sales battered securities. The DJIA experienced an unprecedented drop of approximately 12 percent on Black Tuesday. And Black Tuesday was only the beginning of the troubles. The stock market finally bottomed out on July 8th, 1932. It would not again reach the high figures registered on September 3rd, 1929, until November 23rd, 1954.[20]

The crowd outside the New York Stock Exchange on October 29th, 1929.
https://commons.wikimedia.org/wiki/File:Crowd_outside_nyse.jpg

[19] History.com. (2023, November 16). Stock Market Crash of 1929.

[20] Amadeo, K. (2021, March 4). Black Tuesday, Its Causes and How It Kicked Off the Depression. Retrieved from The balance: https://www.thebalancemoney.com/black-tuesday-definition-cause-kickoff-to-depression-3305819.

Greed is the culprit usually accused for the Great Crash of 1929. Perhaps unrealistic expectations will give one a better understanding of the mood investors had prior to the collapse. People believed that economic prosperity was a given and that things would only get better. They assumed that buying on margin would create extraordinary wealth for them, and that expectation permitted them to take risks they ordinarily would not have. The hope that life would get even better propelled small investors to make big mistakes.

Black Tuesday is often seen as the culmination of a speculative bubble that had been building for years. The crash had far-reaching economic and social consequences, as it marked the beginning of a time of intense suffering and a prolonged period of economic hardship that profoundly affected the United States and the world. The crash of 1929 remains a pivotal moment in financial history and serves as a cautionary tale about the dangers of unchecked speculation and the importance of financial regulation.

Lisbon, the capital of Portugal, was rocked by an earthquake on November 1st, 1755. The event was horrific, but survivors who sought the safety of the port's docks could look out over the waters and watch something more terrible begin to happen. A tidal wave of epic proportions formed off the coast and hit the wrecked city within an hour of the earthquake's shock. The swell was worse than the earthquake.

Stockbrokers and investors finally shook off the dust of the destruction caused by Black Tuesday. However, the end of the day did not mean that the financial condition of the United States was safe. An economic tsunami of historical proportions was forming and would soon crash into America. It was the Great Depression.

Chapter 3: The American Banking System on the Brink

In the years leading up to the infamous Black Tuesday of October 29th, 1929, the American banking system appeared financially strong. The facade of financial robustness, however, masked vulnerabilities and risks that would ultimately contribute to the severity of the Great Depression. To appreciate more completely the dynamics at play when the crash happened, it is essential to delve into the financial landscape of the 1920s and examine the factors that shaped the banks' apparent strength.

<u>Increases in Assets and Diversification</u>

In the 1920s, total banking assets grew significantly, with many banks enjoying substantial increases in deposits and loans. A booming economy caused this, and the growth was fueled by factors such as industrialization, increased consumer spending, and a surge in investment. In 1920, total bank deposits in the United States amounted to approximately $42 billion, and by 1929, this figure had jumped to nearly $58 billion.

American banks diversified their services in the 1920s, offering not only traditional savings and loan functions but also securities trading as well. Some of the largest banks, such as J. P. Morgan & Co., were deeply involved in underwriting stocks and bonds for corporate clients. Banks increased their fee income and profits by expanding the number of services allowed.

The general public firmly believed in the banking system's stability. People were convinced their deposits were secure, and this confidence led to more individual deposits. The notion that "as safe as money in the bank" was deeply ingrained in American culture at the time. Sadly, the confidence was misplaced. There were structural weaknesses behind the mask.

Major Flash Points

The ties of the American banking system to the stock market were frightening. Bankers looked at Wall Street as an opportunity to gain significant profits, and safety measures were ignored. The banks were investing substantial portions of their capital in stocks. Moreover, they were loaning money to customers for stock purposes. This meant that banks were overexposed to the movement of the stock market and its high volatility. A sharp decline in the DJIA could have significant consequences. Yet, chief executives, such as Charles E. Mitchell, president of National City Bank, were encouraging investors to buy stocks.[21]

Overleveraged and Overextended

In a banking environment, "overleveraged" is a situation where a financial institution has borrowed or taken on excessive amounts of debt or leverage relative to its own equity or capital. A large part of a bank's assets or investments are funded with borrowed money instead of its own capital. There is a chance for significant gains, but there is also a chance for dramatic losses. Overleveraging makes a bank vulnerable to adverse market conditions or unexpected events. It can be a devil's bargain.

American banks were heavily involved in the stock market. These financial institutions invested substantial portions of their own capital in stocks and extended loans to customers for stock purchases. There was an excessive amount of bank loans at the time of the market crash that could not be quickly liquidated. The reserves many banks had were not adequate to cover obligations. In addition, banks were not doing a good job of evaluating people's credit risks. Risk management is much more efficient and sophisticated today than it was back in the time of the Great Crash. Financial institutions did not show the attention to detail that

---

[21] Gary Richardson, A. K. (2023, December 23). Stock Market Crash of 1929. Retrieved from Federal Reserve History: https://www.federalreservehistory.org/essays/stock-market-crash-of-1929.

proper risk management requires, and consequently, loans were given to investors who should not have received any funding. Everything seemed to ride on the stock market continuing to be successful.[22]

Poor Regulatory Oversight

Before the Great Crash of 1929, the regulatory oversight of banks in the United States was limited compared to the regulatory framework in place today. The Federal Reserve, created in 1913, did exist, but it had limited power to regulate and supervise the banking sector.

The Federal Reserve Act of 1913 primarily focused on its monetary policy functions, such as controlling the money supply and interest rates. It had the power to set reserve requirements for member banks, but the Federal Reserve lacked comprehensive regulatory authority over all the American banks. Many banks operated with a degree of freedom that allowed them to make risky investments and speculative loans.

The regulation was conducted mainly at the state level. Each state had its own banking department or authority responsible for chartering and supervising state-chartered banks. These state regulators had varying degrees of effectiveness and resources, leading to inconsistent regulatory practices across states.

No federal deposit insurance system existed to protect depositors' funds in the event of a bank failure. If a bank went bankrupt, depositors could lose their entire savings. This encouraged runs on banks, especially as the public lost confidence in the banking system.

Interstate banking was restricted since banks primarily operated within their own states. This limited the potential for large, nationwide financial institutions, but it also limited diversification and spread financial risks across regions.

Overall, the regulatory framework for banks in the 1920s was less developed and less effective in addressing systemic risks compared to today. Disclosure and reporting requirements were also less comprehensive than they are today, making it challenging for regulators and the public to assess banks' financial health accurately.

It is important to note that while the American banking system seemed robust on the surface, these vulnerabilities would become painfully evident when the stock market crashed on Black Tuesday in

---

[22] McGee, S. (2021, May 13). How Bank Failures Contributed to the Great Depression.

1929. Weaknesses and the lack of sound regulatory practices made American banks susceptible to failure and the one phenomenon that every banker dreads: a bank run.

A Mad Dash for Cash

A "run on the bank" happens when a large number of depositors rush to withdraw their funds from a bank within a relatively short period because of concerns about the bank's solvency or a loss of confidence in the financial institution being able to honor withdrawal requests. A run on the bank can lead to a liquidity crisis for a financial institution, as it may not have enough cash on hand to satisfy all the withdrawal demands. This can ultimately result in the bank's insolvency or failure.

Runs on banks occurred during previous financial panics and economic downturns in the United States. These were often triggered by a combination of factors.

- Economic downturns and financial crises eroded public confidence in the banks' stability. When people began to lose their jobs or witnessed a decline in their investments, they became more cautious about the safety of their deposits.
- Sometimes, unfounded rumors or speculation about a bank's financial health could spark a panic. People would hear whispers of potential insolvency or trouble at a bank, which could quickly lead to a rush of depositors trying to withdraw their money.
- During these panics, multiple banks would face runs simultaneously, intensifying the overall financial instability.
- The absence of federal deposit insurance meant that depositors had no guaranteed protection for their savings. If a bank failed, depositors risked losing all their deposits above the limits set by state deposit insurance programs (which varied by state).

A Gathering Crisis of Confidence

The American banking problems in the early months of 1930 were a continuation of the challenges that had emerged in the wake of the stock market crash of 1929. These problems persisted and even intensified during the early months of the new year, contributing to a deepening financial crisis.

The stock market continued to decline, causing further damage to the banks. As the Great Depression deepened, many businesses faced financial difficulties and bankruptcy. President Hoover hoped to prevent panic by ordering federal agencies to speed up construction projects and doubling spending on public works, which included the construction of dams, public buildings, and highways. His efforts were not able to stop the economic downturn, and as the economy soured, more businesses reduced output or declared bankruptcy.

Unemployment began to rise, and economic hardships faced by individuals and families reduced their ability to repay loans. This had a direct impact on banks, as they often held loans and financial interests in these companies. As businesses failed, banks suffered additional losses.[23]

Anxiety started spreading as families were required to use their savings to keep their heads above water. The lack of federal deposit insurance meant that depositors had no guaranteed protection for their savings. The limited deposit insurance programs at the state level offered only partial coverage. Consequently, many depositors risked losing their entire savings. People rushed to withdraw their funds from weak or vulnerable banks, causing a drain of cash reserves from many banks and making it increasingly difficult for them to meet withdrawal demands.

Despite all these problems, there was optimism that the economy was going to recover. There had been three economic contractions in the 1920s, and these lasted for fifteen months on average. One problem that the American banking system faced was that while eight thousand commercial banks belonged to the Federal Reserve System, almost twice that number were not members. Those banks outside of the reserve system were areas of potential disaster. It was going to take a lot of work to mobilize needed cash reserves in the event of systemic bank failures.

The First Shoe

Caldwell and Company was a banking conglomerate headquartered in Nashville, Tennessee. It provided its clients with attractive financial services that included insurance, brokerage, and banking. Caldwell and Company was expanding, but the stock market crash hurt the parent company. Caldwell was heavily invested in securities and lost considerable amounts of money. Company executives drained cash from the banks they controlled to cover the losses, depriving local financial

---

[23] Herbert Hoover Presidential Library and Museum. (2023, December 24). The Great Depression. Retrieved from Hoover.archives.gov: https://hoover.archives.gov/exhibits/great-depression.

institutions of important cash reserves.

A crisis erupted on November 7th, 1930, when a Caldwell subsidiary, the Bank of Tennessee, closed. This was followed on November 12th and 17th when Caldwell affiliates in Louisville, Kentucky, and Knoxville, Tennessee, shut their doors. Commercial banks started to suspend their operations. There was an interconnectedness of banks, with many having loans or financial relationships with one another, which meant that one institution's failure could lead to a ripple effect. The collapse of a single bank could trigger concerns about the stability of other banks, leading to depositor withdrawals and runs.

And that was what happened. Depositors panicked and started to withdraw their money from other banks. Regional banks began to close or suspend operations, and the emergency started to spread beyond rural communities.

The Bank of United States, one of the largest in New York City, closed on December 11th, 1930. The banking crisis spread across the nation, affecting the Sixth District of the Federal Reserve and then the Eighth District. Lending went down, and hundreds of banks failed. Chicago banks began to suffer in June 1931.

The crowd outside the Bank of United States.
https://commons.wikimedia.org/wiki/File:Bank_of_the_United_States_failure_NYWTS.jpg

The subsequent panic and withdrawal of funds by depositors exposed the fragility of the banks, leading to a wave of bank failures and a severe contraction of the money supply, ultimately exacerbating the economic catastrophe of the Great Depression.[24]

An International Banking Crisis

Banking difficulties were not limited to the United States. There were problems overseas that would impact America. There was a crisis in Europe that occurred almost simultaneously with what was happening in the US. The global economic environment was precarious due to the aftermath of World War I and its economic consequences, such as the heavy war debts owed by European nations to the United States. Economies in Europe were struggling to get back on their feet, and many countries were having trouble paying back their debts.

In May 1931, the Creditanstalt, a prominent Austrian bank, faced a severe problem and had to be bailed out. This event sent shockwaves through the international financial system. Later in the year, Germany also experienced a banking crisis when the Danat-Bank and the Landesbank der Rheinprovinz collapsed in July. These crises undermined confidence in European banks and contributed to the broader financial crisis.

As economic conditions deteriorated, bank runs and withdrawals became more frequent overseas. People and institutions rushed to withdraw their deposits from banks, fearing that their savings might be lost if banks collapsed. This mass withdrawal of funds placed additional strain on the already fragile banking systems.

Gold Standard Issues

Under the gold standard, a country's central bank is limited in its ability to use monetary policy tools to respond to economic crises. Since the value of the currency was tied to a fixed quantity of gold, central banks had to maintain a certain amount of gold reserves. The gold standard's rigidity, combined with a commitment to maintaining a fixed exchange rate between currency and a specific quantity of gold, caused trouble during the Great Depression. The constraints restricted a country's ability to expand the money supply, lower interest rates, or use other measures to stimulate the economy during the Great Depression. The gold standard also promoted exchange rate stability at the expense of domestic economic strength. When a country experienced financial difficulties, it could not devalue its currency to make its exports more

---

[24] Richardson, G. (2023, December 24). Banking Panics of 1930-31. Retrieved from Federal Reserve History: https://www.federalreservehistory.org/essays/banking-panics-1930-31.

competitive or reduce the debt burden.

To address these challenges, several countries, including the United Kingdom and other European nations, made the difficult decision to abandon the gold standard in 1931. This decision was prompted by the need to implement expansionary monetary policies to combat the economic crisis. However, the abandonment of the gold standard also contributed to a loss of confidence in currencies, as it signaled that the gold standard's stability had been compromised.

The banking crisis brought on deflation, as banks and the public started to hoard cash, depriving banks of the capital required to build reserves or finance loans. Consumption fell, and with a loss of consumer demand came a rise in unemployment.

In summary, the years 1930 and 1931 marked a continuation of the banking problems that surfaced following the stock market crash of 1929. Bank failures, depositor panic, the lack of deposit insurance, and the broader economic challenges associated with the Great Depression all contributed to the ongoing turmoil in the American banking system. These problems would persist and worsen in the years that followed.

Chapter 4: The Dust Bowl and Agriculture Issues

"American Gothic," painted by Grant Wood, is an iconic painting of the Great Depression. The man and woman represented in the artwork are intended to represent the values and resilience of the American farmland. Rural America's residents needed all the courage and determination they could muster during the Great Depression. The American farmer was severely tested by the economic disruption of that time.

The Farm

In the early 1930s, American agriculture was in a state of crisis. The Great Depression had taken a heavy toll on the nation's rural areas, where farming was a way of life for many. According to the 1930 Census of Distribution, nearly sixty-five million Americans lived in small urban areas consisting of fewer than ten thousand people and open country. This rural population relied heavily on farming for their livelihoods, and the economic hardship of the Great Depression hit them hard. Falling agricultural prices, droughts, and soil erosion made it almost impossible for many farmers to make a living. Thousands of farmers were pushed into bankruptcy and foreclosure. These hardships had far-reaching consequences for the rural areas and for the rest of the country as well.

Commodity Prices

The financial health of a rural area depended on commodity prices. How much a crop will sell for can determine whether a farmer is successful or is faced with possible bankruptcy. American farmers enjoyed unprecedented prosperity during World War I, when armies relied heavily on the food farmers produced. Prices were relatively high after the war since the European demand for American crops was high. The good years were followed by lean times, with surpluses causing produce prices to go down.[25]

Parts of farm country lacked crop diversification, so the market performance of a particular commodity held a dominant influence over one's prosperity. Several essential agricultural commodities faced severe price troubles during this period.

Wheat prices fell dramatically during the early years of the Great Depression. Overproduction led to a surplus of wheat and a sharp drop in prices. Many wheat farmers needed help to cover their production costs. Corn prices were also severely affected by the Depression. Corn faced overproduction issues, and farmers had to contend with low prices that made it difficult to make ends meet.

The dominance of a commodity in a region could seriously impact the welfare of thousands. The South was especially vulnerable to the whims of the commodity market, where tobacco and cotton were the mainstays of the economy. The American cotton crop yielded $1.5 billion in 1929, which fell to $465 million in 1932. Cigarette tobacco crop receipts realized in 1932 were only a third of the figures realized in 1929.[26]

<u>Farm Financing</u>

Farming in the United States in 1930 was financed through a combination of methods and sources, but it was a challenging time for many farmers due to the economic hardships of the Great Depression.

Many farmers relied on their own savings, assets, and income from their farms to finance their operations. This included using profits from previous years' harvests to cover current expenses and investments in seeds, equipment, and labor. Bank loans for essentials such as fertilizer,

[25] Encylcopedia.com. (2023, December 24). Farm Relief 1929-1941. Retrieved from Encyclopedia.com: https://www.encyclopedia.com/education/news-and-education-magazines/farm-relief-1929-1941.

[26] Encylcopedia.com. (2023, December 24). Great Depression in the South. Retrieved from Encylopedia.com: https://www.encyclopedia.com/economics/encyclopedias-almanacs-transcripts-and-maps/south-great-depression.

seed, and machinery would be sought. The Federal Farm Loan Act of 1916 established a federal land bank system, which provided farmers with long-term, low-interest loans. These banks were part of the Farm Credit System and aimed to make credit more accessible to agricultural borrowers. Farmers could use these loans for land purchases, farm improvements, and debt refinancing. Tenant farmers did not own their land. These people, along with sharecroppers, relied heavily on the financial success of a crop in order to stay solvent.

Loan collateral was either the future crop or the land the farmer owned. The collapse of commodity prices made it increasingly more difficult for farmers to repay their loans. This only added to the general misery of people living in rural areas.

The Rise of Foreclosure

Farm foreclosures in the United States during the years 1930 to 1932 were distressingly extensive. There was a wave of foreclosures that impacted farmers across the country. Many farmers were unable to make payments on their loans. The banking crisis of the early 1930s caused many banks to close. As banks failed, farmers lost access to credit, making it even more challenging for them to secure the money required to continue operations or pay off existing debts.

Farm foreclosures became a routine feature of life. Hundreds of thousands of farmers lost the title to property that had been in their families for generations. The problem had started in the 1920s, but it metastasized during the early days of the Great Depression. The average foreclosure rate on American farms between 1913 and 1920 was 3.2 per 1,000 farms. This figure grew to 17.4 per 1,000 farms. In 1926, it reached 38.8 per 1,000 farms by 1933. That year was catastrophic; over 200,000 farms were foreclosed on.[27]

Southern states were among the most brutally hit. What happened in one tobacco county in North Carolina is a significant example of what happened. This area of the state had 3,500 foreclosures on the county's 5,280 farms.[28]

---

[27] Encylcopedia.com. (2023, December 24). Farm Foreclosures. Retrieved from Encyclopedia.com: https://www.encyclopedia.com/economics/encyclopedias-almanacs-transcripts-and-maps/farm-foreclosures.

[28] Encylcopedia.com. (2023, December 24). Great Depression in the South.

Public auctions were held to sell the foreclosed property. These gave rise to "penny auctions." Farmers who attended auctions placed incredibly low bids on the land, and few were brave enough to bid any higher.

Farmers protested by blocking foreclosure sales. Anger and frustration were the primary emotions in American agriculture, and the environment was about to make things worse.

The Dust Bowl

The Dust Bowl was a period of severe environmental and agricultural issues that occurred in the United States during the 1930s. Devastating dust storms, soil erosion, and agricultural failures took place in the Great Plains region of the country. It remains one of most significant environmental disasters in United States history.

The most intense dust storms happened between 1931 and 1939. The areas impacted included parts of the states of Oklahoma, Texas, Kansas, Colorado, New Mexico, Nebraska, South Dakota, and North Dakota. There was also devastation recorded in Arkansas, Missouri, and Iowa. Major dust storms, sometimes called "black blizzards," overwhelmed the land. Enormous clouds of fine soil particles blotted out the sun and traveled hundreds of miles.

These dust storms were disastrous for agriculture, health, and the environment. The Dust Bowl led to the widespread failure of crops, killing livestock and causing economic hardship for farmers and communities. Many farmers lost their farms and homes, causing them to leave the area where they grew up to seek better opportunities elsewhere.

Causes of the Disaster

The Great Plains is a naturally dry environment that does not get much rain. The 1930s was exceptionally dry. There was a recorded drop in rainfall in the area between 1932 and 1939. As mentioned, the Great Plains experienced an unusual number of dust storms, with fourteen notable occurrences in 1932 and thirty-eight in 1938. The force of these storms was strong enough to carry topsoil thousands of miles away. That happened on May 11th, 1934. A two-mile-high dust storm moved to the East Coast, blocking the view of the US Capitol Building. The worst storm hit on April 14th, 1935. A towering wall of sand and dust from

Oklahoma roared eastward and blew millions of tons of topsoil with it.[29]

Buried machinery during the Dust Bowl.
https://commons.wikimedia.org/wiki/File:Dust_Bowl_-_Dallas,_South_Dakota_1936.jpg

A significant factor that led to the calamity was the farming practices of the time. Many farmers in the Great Plains were encouraged to practice farming techniques that did not consider soil conservation. The Great Plains region had vast areas of grassland that were plowed up for farming, which exposed the soil to erosion by wind and water. Strong winds could carry away topsoil because there were no prairie grasses to hold the ground in place.[30]

Farmers plowed deep and did not rotate their crops, leaving the soil susceptible to erosion. Farmers also lacked access to modern soil conservation techniques and tools. Contour farming, crop rotation, and terracing, which can mitigate soil erosion, were not widely adopted. Overgrazing livestock, especially cattle and sheep, contributed to vegetation depletion and the exposure of bare soil. This made the land

---

[29] Science.Smith. (2023, December 24). The Dust Bowl (c.1930-1940). Retrieved from Science.Smith.edu: https://www.science.smith.edu/climatelit/the-dust-bowl/.

[30] Editors, H. (2023, April 24). Dust Bowl. Retrieved from History.com: https://www.history.com/topics/great-depression/dust-bowl.

more disposed to erosion during the drought and windy conditions.

The economic hardships put significant pressure on farmers to produce more crops. They often tried to cultivate land that was not suited for large-scale farming, which only served to worsen the soil erosion.

The Worst Hit Areas

Oklahoma was the epicenter of the Dust Bowl. This state experienced some of the most severe dust storms and soil erosion. The "Okies," a term used to describe migrants from Oklahoma and neighboring states who were displaced by the Dust Bowl, became one of the most recognizable groups of people affected by the disaster. Texas also experienced significant dust storms and drought conditions during the Dust Bowl. Kansas also greatly suffered from severe soil erosion and dust storms.

A mother and her children living in a shanty in Oklahoma.

Southeastern Colorado was affected by the dust storms and drought. Poor land management and adverse weather conditions led to significant agricultural losses. Parts of eastern and southeastern New Mexico were also damaged by dust storms and drought. Agricultural productivity declined sharply in these regions.

Although Nebraska was not as severely affected as some other states, it still experienced dust storms and drought conditions during the Dust Bowl. The Dakotas also experienced dust storms and soil erosion, but the impact was somewhat less severe compared to states farther south.[31]

The Okie Migration

The human cost was the most dramatic price exacted by the Dust Bowl and the failures of agriculture. Farmers realized the chances of growing crops were slim or nonexistent without that precious layer of topsoil. Many believed they had to leave and seek opportunities elsewhere. The Okie migration was perhaps the worst tragedy of the Great Depression.

The Dust Bowl forced thousands of families in the southern Great Plains to undertake a massive migration. The Oklahoma Panhandle, including Cimarron, Texas, and Beaver counties, was among the areas most severely affected by the Dust Bowl. The Panhandle experienced relentless dust storms, extreme drought, and severe soil erosion, leading to the collapse of agriculture.

While precise numbers are difficult to ascertain, some estimates suggest that between 300,000 and 400,000 Oklahomans moved from their homes. An estimated 250,000 Oklahomans moved to California from 1935 to 1940, and a third of those migrants settled in the San Joaquin Valley.[32]

The Human Cost

The Okie migration led to profound hardships and challenges for those who were forced to leave their homes in search of a better life.

[31] Cassidy, D. (2022, August 6). Weather Wonders: The Dust Bowl. Retrieved from KWWL.com: https://www.kwwl.com/weather/blog/weather-wonders-the-dust-bowl/article_5ad85530-079c-11ed-9e6d-77fc5127444e.html.

[32] Wilhite, D. A. (2023, December 24). The Encyclopedia of Oklahoma History and Culture: Dust Bowl. Retrieved from Oklahoma Historical Society: https://www.okhistory.org/publications/enc/entry.php?entry=DU011#:~:text=As%20a%20result%2C%20dust%20storms,Colorado%20and%20northeastern%20New%20Mexico.

Families were often torn apart, as some members left to seek employment in distant states while others remained behind. Separation from loved ones caused emotional strain and disrupted the traditional family structure.

Forced relocations created health consequences as well. The harsh living conditions during the migration, such as overcrowded makeshift camps, exposure to the elements, and inadequate sanitation, led to health issues. Respiratory problems and "dust pneumonia" were common due to exposure to dust storms. Malnutrition and insufficient access to healthcare further exacerbated health problems.

Farmers lost their homes, farms, and possessions due to bank foreclosures, making them destitute. Okies struggled to find work, and when they did, it was usually in low-paying, labor-intensive jobs. Children often faced interrupted schooling as their families moved frequently in search of work. The lack of stable education had long-term implications for their academic and career prospects. Economic instability persisted for years, and families had difficulty recovering from the financial losses incurred during the Dust Bowl.

John Steinbeck's classic *The Grapes of Wrath* graphically portrayed the prejudice the Okies faced as they searched for financial and social stability. Okie migrants faced discrimination in their new destinations, particularly in California. They were blamed for taking jobs and straining local resources.

Okies were often seen as outsiders in their new locations. Migrants faced challenges integrating into new communities due to cultural differences and prejudices. The breakdown of social networks and support systems further isolated individuals and families. Depression, anxiety, and a sense of hopelessness were frequent problems, and they took a toll on people's mental health.

However, the migration also demonstrated the strength and adaptability of those who endured these difficult days, leaving behind a lasting legacy of resilience and perseverance.

The government did not stand idly by and watch as the human cost of the Great Depression mounted. Solutions to the problems were desperately being sought. Unfortunately, some of the corrective actions were outdated. America had never seen problems like this since the Civil War. The traditional ways of solving economic problems would not be satisfactory enough to get the country back on its feet. Innovation was necessary, and new methods had to be tried. The changes had to come as soon as possible.

Americans have proven time and time again that they have considerable resilience and patience, but these qualities start to wear thin as bad times linger and refuse to leave. The Great Depression was a challenge that had to be met and conquered quickly before unacceptable social changes warped the American nation.

Chapter 5: The Government's Response: Herbert Hoover

The government actively tried to respond to the crisis. Herbert Hoover was the president of the United States during the darkest days of the Great Depression. He had the enormous responsibility of bringing things back to a sense of normal. There were sustained efforts to correct the problems that were surfacing and to bring relief to those who were suffering.

Critics accused Herbert Hoover of not doing enough and said he was insensitive to the plight of the ordinary people. Those are unfair accusations; history has shown that Hoover worked to make things better.

Herbert Hoover.
https://commons.wikimedia.org/wiki/File:President_Hoover_portrait.jpg

Previous Successes

Hoover saved hundreds of thousands of lives prior to becoming president. He had a distinguished career in public service, particularly during and after World War I. He was prominent in leading and organizing relief efforts domestically and internationally. The notable relief programs and organizations that Hoover was involved in before his presidency included the following:

- Relief efforts for stranded Americans: Thousands of American citizens fled continental Europe at the start of World War I and took refuge in the United Kingdom. Unfortunately, these refugees lacked the resources to get back home to the United States. Hoover helped organize emergency relief that provided temporary shelter, food, and financial assistance to those Americans who were in a strange land.

- Commission for Relief in Belgium (CRB): Hoover played a significant role in organizing the Commission for Relief in Belgium (CRB) during World War I. The CRB was a neutral organization that aimed to provide food and relief to the people of Belgium who were suffering from food shortages and famine due to the war. Hoover's success in this endeavor earned him a reputation as a skilled organizer and humanitarian.

- American Relief Administration (ARA): Hoover led the ARA, which was established in 1919, to provide food aid and humanitarian relief to war-torn Europe, particularly in the aftermath of World War I and during the Russian famine, which lasted from 1921 to 1923. The ARA eventually fed almost eleven million Russians per day in nineteen thousand kitchens. Hoover's leadership in this role earned him international recognition and praise for his efforts to alleviate suffering and provide relief to millions of people.

Hoover's biographer, George Nash, discussed Hoover's achievements. He summarized the legacy President Hoover left behind:

"Hoover was really the vanguard of the whole approach that has become associated with America in the last hundred years, namely that when there is a humanitarian tragedy in the world, whether from war or famine or revolution or a typhoon or earthquake, the Americans will be there to organize the relief."[33]

Hoover's prior experience in relief efforts shaped his public image. His work in various organizations showcased his ability to coordinate large-scale relief operations effectively. The man was certainly qualified to lead efforts to help people trapped in a financial disaster.

Early Efforts in the Great Depression

In the first days of the Great Depression, Herbert Hoover took several measures to address the economic crisis. He tried to boost confidence in the economy by delivering speeches and making public statements that stressed the need for optimism and a belief in the strength of the American economy. He was convinced a positive attitude would help stabilize the situation.

An immediate response to the Great Depression was the President's Emergency Committee for Employment (PECE). It was organized by Hoover in October 1930 and tasked with activities intended to correct the bleak economic situation. The committee's objective was proactive efforts, including the following:

- Promote employment opportunities: The committee sought to promote and expand employment opportunities for American workers. It recognized the need to generate more jobs in a time of economic hardship and to find ways to stimulate economic activity.

- Address unemployment and economic distress: With unemployment rates rising during the early years of the Great Depression, the PECE aimed to alleviate economic distress by addressing unemployment at both the national and local levels. It encouraged local communities to engage in projects that would create jobs.

- Stabilize the economy: Another objective of the PECE was to stabilize the US economy. It sought to restore confidence in the financial system and promote stability in the business environment.

- Encourage voluntary cooperation: The PECE encouraged voluntary cooperation between the government and industries

---

[33] National Park Service. (2023, December 24). The Emergence of the Great Humanitarian. Retrieved from NPS.gov: https://www.nps.gov/articles/emergence-of-the-great-humanitarian.htm.

to address the growing unemployment crisis. It brought together representatives from various sectors of the economy, including business leaders, labor unions, and government officials, to collaborate on strategies to combat unemployment.

The president was willing to use public works projects to address the unemployment situation. In December 1930, Hoover asked for $100 million from Congress to pay for a program of public works that included the construction of highways, public buildings, and improvements to rivers and harbors. He also used moral persuasion to encourage employers to keep employees on the job.[34]

Dealing with the Financial Crisis

Hoover did more than promote public works projects. He cut taxes and declared a moratorium on the payment of international debt. The Reconstruction Finance Corporation (RFC) was created in January 1932 to help American banks and businesses. The Emergency Relief and Construction Act was passed into law in July 1932, which increased the RFC's lending authority to include financing state and local public works.

Hoover recognized the problems faced by farmers by approving increases in farm subsidies. He set up the Federal Home Loan Bank Board to support mortgages. Although Hoover did raise taxes to pay for programs, they were estate taxes and corporate taxes; he also increased the top personal tax rate to 63 percent. The rich and corporate America would have to pay their fair share before others were asked to pay more.[35]

Hoover's initial efforts to end the crisis were praised, but the Great Depression was more than just a limited financial crisis. Each year of the Hoover administration brought on a new emergency and problems to be addressed. There is no question that the president tried. However, there were some flaws in his approach to correcting the situation that limited the effectiveness of his programs. What began as an appreciation for his attempts became harsh criticism and the growing belief that Herbert Hoover did not know what to do.

---

[34] U-S-history.com. (2023, December 24). Hoover's Early Relief Efforts. Retrieved from U-S-history.com: https://www.u-s-history.com/pages/h1533.html.

[35] Klein, C. (2023, September 26). Before FDR, Herbert Hoover Tred His Own "New Deal." Retrieved from History.com: https://www.history.com/news/great-depression-herbert-hoover-new-deal.

A Problem of Perception

History has not been kind to Herbert Hoover. Members of the Roosevelt administration promoted the idea that Hoover was insensitive to the common man's plight. There is little evidence to support the story of a cold-hearted president. A perception issue was probably at fault.

Hoover believed in limited government intervention. He thought the economy would eventually self-correct and that the government should not play an overly active role in economic affairs. Others felt the same way. Treasury Secretary Andrew Mellon was also convinced that the government should not play a significant role.[36]

Hoover's early successes were centered around persuading people to take an active role in helping their fellow citizens. Appeals to civic spirit had saved millions from starvation during and after World War I. Consequently, Hoover's administration did not immediately implement widespread direct relief programs for individuals and families suffering from unemployment and poverty. The president believed that voluntary charity organizations and local relief efforts could adequately address the problem. Hoover encouraged individuals and communities to support charities and local relief efforts to help the needy. However, these efforts were insufficient to meet the need.

Hoover wanted to maintain a balanced federal budget. While fiscal responsibility is generally sound economic policy, the insistence on balancing the budget during a financial crisis reduced government spending and increased taxation, further aggravated economic problems. Hoover eventually raised government spending and increased federal expenditures by 48 percent during his presidency. (Interestingly, during the 1932 presidential election, Franklin Roosevelt accused him of "reckless and extravagant" spending.)

Initially, Hoover underestimated the depth and severity of the Great Depression. He viewed it as a cyclical downturn that would be temporary and self-correcting. This initial misjudgment delayed his response to the crisis, allowing it to worsen.

---

[36] U-S-history.com. (2023, December 24). Hoover's Early Relief Efforts. Retrieved from U-S-history.com: https://www.u-s-history.com/pages/h1533.html.

During his presidency, there was a severe banking and financial crisis, with numerous bank failures and a collapsing financial system. Over five thousand banks failed during Hoover's time in office, and the unemployment rate rose from 3 percent to 25 percent.[37]

In fairness to Hoover, much of what happened in the early 1930s was unprecedented. The comprehensive nature of the Great Depression meant there were too many fires to put out, and the traditional means of correcting the situation were not doing the job. Clearly, though, there were areas where Hoover's efforts were the wrong remedy.

• Unemployment Missteps

Hoover tried to stem the growth of unemployment, but his policy decisions could have been better. He called upon businesses, labor unions, and local communities to voluntarily take measures to prevent layoffs and reduce wage cuts. He hoped that employers and workers would cooperate to stabilize employment and wages. However, those efforts were not enough.

He advocated for increased construction and public works projects, but he also relied more on local and state governments to fund and implement these efforts. They would prove to be limited in scale.[38]

Two Significant Blunders

There are two situations where Hoover's actions or responses to an emergency were utterly wrong. One was a significant mistake in financial policy, and the other was a public relations disaster.

The Smoot-Hawley Tariff Act

The Smoot-Hawley Tariff Act, officially known as the Tariff Act of 1930, was signed into law by the president in June 1930. While its primary intention was to protect American industries and agriculture during the Great Depression, it is regarded as a disastrous policy that exacerbated the economic challenges of the time and contributed to the severity of the Great Depression. It backfired horribly.

The Smoot-Hawley Tariff Act substantially raised tariffs on many imported goods, effectively levying high taxes on foreign products entering the United States. The rise in trade barriers was meant to

[37] Klein, C. (2023, September 26). Before FDR, Herbert Hoover Tred His Own "New Deal."

[38] Digital History. (2023, December 24). President Hoover. Retrieved from Digital History.uh.edu: https://www.digitalhistory.uh.edu/disp_textbook.cfm?smtID=2&psid=3436.

protect American industries from foreign competition, but there were negative consequences.

The higher tariffs resulted in increased prices for imported goods, which, in turn, raised living costs for American consumers. This reduction in consumer purchasing power further hampered economic recovery. The Smoot-Hawley Tariff triggered retaliation from other countries. Many trading partners imposed their own retaliatory tariffs on American goods. This tit-for-tat trade war further reduced international trade and exports, harming those American industries that relied on foreign markets.[39]

The tariff increase significantly reduced international trade, which was already suffering due to the global economic downturn. Reduced trade had a detrimental effect on American exports and contributed to a decline in the manufacturing and agricultural sectors. It also eroded international and domestic confidence in American economic policies. Foreign nations viewed the Smoot-Hawley Tariff Act as a protectionist measure that hindered global economic recovery efforts, and domestic businesses and consumers felt the negative economic consequences.

While the tariff aimed to protect American agriculture, it hurt farmers instead. Agricultural exports fell sharply due to retaliatory tariffs imposed by trading partners, causing agricultural prices to plummet and leading to widespread rural distress.[40]

The tariff did not help American industries; it had the opposite effect, contributing to the severity and duration of the economic downturn. It is a primary example of the unintended consequences of protectionist trade policies during times of financial crisis.

The Bonus Army March

The march on Washington by World War I veterans, also known as the Bonus Army March, occurred in the summer of 1932. The impact on public opinion was extreme, and Hoover's image would not recover.

---

[39] Team, C. (2023, December 24). Smoot-Hawley Tariff Act. Retrieved from Corporatefinancenstitute.com: https://corporatefinanceinstitute.com/resources/economics/smoot-hawley-tariff-act/.

[40] Theodore Phalan, D. Y. (2012, February 29). The Smoot-Hawley Tariff and the Great Depression. Retrieved from Fee.org: https://fee.org/articles/the-smoot-hawley-tariff-and-the-great-depression/.

Congress passed the World War Adjusted Compensation Act in 1924, which gave bonuses to World War I veterans as a deferred payment for their service to America. The bonuses were not payable until 1945. However, as the Great Depression deepened, many veterans faced dire economic circumstances and began demanding early payment of their bonuses to provide immediate financial relief. Thousands of World War I veterans began converging on Washington, DC, in May 1932 to press for the immediate payment of those bonuses. They established makeshift camps near the US Capitol Flats.

The Bonus Army organized peaceful protests and marches in Washington, DC, to draw attention to their cause. As the number of protesters grew, tensions escalated between the veterans and authorities. President Herbert Hoover ordered the evacuation of the Bonus Army's main camp on the Anacostia Flats, leading to a confrontation with police and the US Army.

The Army, under the command of General Douglas MacArthur, forcibly evicted the Bonus Army from their camp in July 1932. The troops used bayonets and tear gas to clear the camp, which resulted in injuries and some deaths. The use of force against these veterans and their families garnered Hoover a negative public perception.

The burning of Anacostia Flats.
https://commons.wikimedia.org/wiki/File:Evictbonusarmy.jpg

President Hoover's handling of the Bonus Army march had a detrimental effect on his reputation. Many Americans viewed his decision to use military force against veterans as heavy-handed and unsympathetic, further eroding his support during the Great Depression.

While the Bonus Army did not achieve its immediate goal of receiving early payment of their bonuses, the event did contribute to increased pressure on the federal government to provide relief to veterans and the broader population. Congress eventually passed the Adjusted Compensation Payment Act in 1936 during Franklin Roosevelt's first term in office, which authorized the early payment of bonuses.

The eviction of the Bonus Army and the subsequent negative publicity added to the overall climate of unrest during the Great Depression. It highlighted the desperation and suffering of many Americans and underscored the need for more significant government intervention to address the problem.

The Bonus Army March was the last straw. Hoover's response cemented his image in Americans' minds as an uncaring individual who was insensitive to the needs of millions of Americans. However, since we have the benefit of hindsight, we can see that is not true. Nevertheless, the damage was done. Hoover could not resurrect his tattered image, and there were only a few months before the general election. His time in office was coming to an end.

A more comprehensive government intervention and relief program would be necessary to address the issues of the Great Depression. This task fell to Herbert Hoover's successor, Franklin D. Roosevelt. Dramatic action was going to be necessary. Roosevelt needed to do more than make promises to the American people. There was a sense of desperation combined with real anger felt by Americans in all walks of life. American democracy was in grave peril as 1933 began, and policy failures would not be accepted.

Chapter 6: Life during the Great Depression

Those with parents or grandparents who lived during the Great Depression have heard life stories from those times. Those days were defining moments in the lives of many Americans, shaping people's character and defining their personal outlooks on life. The Great Depression challenged the average person in subtle and obvious ways. Some vestiges of those haunting times remain, provided by the art, literature, and music of the time.

<u>Modern Life in the 1930s</u>

The most immediate and visible impact of the Great Depression was the widespread loss of jobs. The unemployment rate reached 25.6 percent in May 1933, putting nearly fifteen million people out of work. Consumer spending and investment plummeted, causing many businesses and factories to close. People from all walks of life found themselves suddenly unemployed. Savings were imperiled as medium-sized banks were forced to close.[41]

---

[41] Pettinger, T. (2020, April 1). Unemployment during the Great Depression. Retrieved from Economic help: https://www.economicshelp.org/blog/162985/economics/unemployment-during-the-great-depression/.

<u>A Family Crisis</u>

Families often struggled to make ends meet, with many falling into poverty. Families struggled to pay mortgages or rent, leading to housing insecurity and evictions. Many families were forced to find alternative living arrangements, including moving in with relatives. Some lost their homes and became homeless.

Access to food was a significant concern for many during the Depression. Food prices went down, but incomes dropped even more, so it was hard to afford basic necessities. Food scarcity and malnutrition were common, and families relied on soup kitchens and charitable organizations for assistance. Small kitchen gardens proliferated. Local communities allowed vacant lots to be converted into "thrift gardens," where people could grow their own food. These programs became larger as the crisis continued. The thrift garden program in Detroit eventually provided food for nearly twenty thousand people.

A line outside a soup kitchen in Chicago.

Marriages were strained, but divorce rates fell because couples could not afford the legal process. Abandoning one's family was known as the "poor man's divorce." Suicide rates skyrocketed.[42]

Healthcare and Education

As poverty rose, there was a decline in sanitation and hygiene in the inner cities and rural areas. However, the public health movement had some successes during the Great Depression. This was because of the New Deal programs, which promoted health and sanitation improvements. Cases of childhood diseases, such as measles, scarlet fever, whooping cough, and diphtheria, dropped significantly. Government programs heightened public health awareness. Quarantines, vaccinations, and sanitary water suppressed once common epidemics.[43]

People could no longer pay their property taxes, which caused budget cutbacks in public schools. Lack of sufficient funds caused a reduction of school hours, and increased class sizes created serious challenges. Teacher salaries were cut, and poor districts in rural areas were forced to close their doors. Black students, in particular, were seriously impacted by these economic cutbacks.

However, like public health, there were success stories during the Great Depression. State funding increased, and school systems combined smaller schools to become more efficient. The curriculum was standardized, and teaching standards for professionals were improved. Education was looked upon as a right and not a luxury. By 1939, there was an increased public demand for governmental support of education.[44]

Hoovervilles

Documentaries about developing countries often show large shanty towns on the outskirts of major cities. They appear as decrepit and hopeless areas of poverty. Something comparable happened in America;

[42] Konkel, L. (2023, January 20). Life for the Average Family during the Great Depression. Retrieved from History.com: https://www.history.com/news/life-for-the-average-family-during-the-great-depression.

[43] Encyclopedia.com. (2023, December 25). Public Health 1929-1941. Retrieved from Encyclopedia.com: https://www.encyclopedia.com/education/news-and-education-magazines/public-health-1929-1941.

[44] Encyclopedia.com. (2023, December 25). Education 1929-1941. Retrieved from Encyclopedia.com: https://www.encyclopedia.com/education/news-and-education-magazines/education-1929-1941.

in fact, it was a characteristic of the Great Depression. These American shantytowns were called Hoovervilles.

Hoovervilles were makeshift, often sordid settlements that emerged during the Great Depression in the United States. They were named after President Herbert Hoover, who was widely criticized for his perceived ineffectual response to the economic hardships of the era. These settlements were primarily inhabited by homeless and impoverished individuals and families.

Hoovervilles were relatively common during the Great Depression, particularly during the early years of the crisis. They were most prevalent in urban areas, especially in large cities, where unemployment rates were high. People had also migrated to cities in search of work, and when they couldn't find any, they were forced to make camp in a Hooverville.

The number of people living in Hoovervilles varied from one settlement to another. Some were relatively small, housing only a few dozen individuals or families, while larger ones could have hundreds or even thousands of residents.

Major cities like New York, Chicago, Los Angeles, and Seattle had significant Hooverville populations. Saint Louis, Missouri, was the largest, and the Hooverville in Seattle, Washington, covered nine acres and housed close to 1,200 people.[45]

Hoovervilles were characterized by huts constructed from scavenged materials, such as cardboard, scrap wood, and tar paper. Basic amenities were scarce, and these shacks were cold in the winter. It was also not easy to keep the rain out. Saturation conditions were terrible, and there was not enough clean drinking water. These conditions caused diseases to spread.

Local governments often viewed Hoovervilles as a problem and sometimes tried to clear them out or relocate the residents. In some cases, charitable organizations and individuals provided food and other assistance to Hooverville residents.

Hoovervilles became symbols of the economic suffering and poverty experienced by many Americans during the Great Depression. They

[45] Longley, R. (2020, May 26). Hoovervilles: Homeless Camps of the Great Depression. Retrieved from ThoughtCo.com: https://www.thoughtco.com/hoovervilles-homeless-camps-of-the-great-depression-4845996.

were a visible manifestation of the failure of the government and the economic system to provide for the population's basic needs.

The Great Migration

Americans were on the move during the Great Depression. Economic conditions at home were so severe that people had to find work elsewhere. This included traveling hundreds or even thousands of miles to find a job. In search of employment and better opportunities, many embarked on journeys. The "Dust Bowl migration" went to states like California. This mass movement contributed to the growth of urban populations in the West.

These were not journeys for pleasure. Instead, they were desperate moves made by desperate people seeking an answer to a problem that was not easily solved. Americans were anxiously looking for a way to improve their economic condition, and taking to the road was one of the ways they tried.

Hobos

During the darkest days of the Great Depression, a peculiar subculture emerged across the United States—hobos. These itinerant wanderers had been around before the Depression, but they came to represent a definite niche in the mass migration that happened as Americans sought to escape economic hardship.

Hobos were predominantly men who left their homes and families to embark on a nomadic lifestyle in search of employment, adventure, or simply survival. Hobos were typically the victims of the economic downturn, losing their jobs, homes, and sense of security. Many of them were displaced workers, former farmers, or drifters who roamed the country's vast rail network. They were distinguishable from other groups of homeless individuals by their choice to travel and their embrace of a specific culture.

Some hobos were motivated by a sense of adventure. They saw the open road as an opportunity to explore, meet new people, and have a life free from the constraints of conventional society. The transient nature of hobo life allowed some to escape legal troubles or debts in their hometowns. Moving from place to place made it difficult for authorities to track them down.

The primary mode of transportation for hobos was the freight train. They would hop on to passing trains and ride the rails to their desired destinations. The journey was dangerous and uncomfortable. Hobos risked injury, arrest, and death while moving around.

Hobos were characterized by their constant movement. They had no permanent home and traveled widely across the country. Despite their roving lives, hobos formed a tight-knit community. They developed their own code of conduct and ethics, including rules about sharing food and shelter and respecting one another's belongings.[46]

These travelers used a system of drawings and pictures to communicate with each other. The pictographs were usually drawn with chalk, making them easy to change when circumstances made it necessary.

Hobo symbols were a testament to the resourcefulness and sense of community that defined the hobo subculture during the Great Depression. They allowed hobos to navigate the challenges of their nomadic lifestyle by sharing information and supporting each other on their journeys along the rails. Below are some common examples of hobo symbols and their meanings:

- No Go (X with a circle around it): The "No Go" symbol warned hobos that the area was unwelcoming or dangerous. It could signify hostile residents, aggressive law enforcement, or other hazards.
- Food Available (Triangle): The triangle symbol represented the promise of food. It was often found near homes or farms where hobos could ask for or scavenge meals.
- Need a Doctor (A plus sign or cross): Hobos used this symbol to request medical assistance or indicate that they were injured and required help.
- Kind Woman (A smiling woman's face): This indicated that a compassionate and generous woman lived there. Hobos could ask for food, shelter, or assistance without fear of rejection.
- Get Out Fast (Wavy Lines): The wavy lines warned that hobos needed to leave the area quickly due to impending danger or law enforcement.

---

[46] National Security Agency/Central Security Service. (2021, August 4). Hobo Communications: A Brief History of Hobos and Their Signs. Retrieved from Nsa.gov: https://www.nsa.gov/History/National-Cryptologic-Museum/Exhibits-Artifacts/Exhibit-View/Article/2718897/hobo-communications-a-brief-history-of-hobos-and-their-signs/.

Other signs would let hobos know if they were welcome in a community or if the police were hostile.[47]

Significant Movements of People

A significant migration of the Great Depression was the movement of African Americans from the Deep South to the North. This was a continuation of the Great Migration that started before World War I. African Americans had long endured racial segregation, economic inequality, and physical violence in the South. The economic turmoil and the promise of better opportunities caused them to leave the oppressive conditions of the South in search of jobs and a chance at a better life. Many were sharecroppers, tenant farmers, or laborers trapped in poverty and discrimination. They were predominantly Black, but some were also of mixed racial heritage.

In the South, Jim Crow laws enforced segregation and racial discrimination. African Americans faced systemic racism, including limited access to education, healthcare, and economic opportunities. The South was plagued by racial violence and lynching. Migration was a way of escaping the constant threat of terror.

There were pockets of economic growth in the North despite the poverty of the Great Depression, especially in urban centers. The automobile industry in Detroit attracted many African Americans in search of factory jobs. Ford Motor's Rouge Factory complex allowed the African American middle class to grow substantially. Nearly 120,000 African Americans lived in the Detroit metropolitan area by 1930.[48]

Chicago became a major destination for African American migrants due to its thriving industrial economy. The city's steel mills, meatpacking plants, and other industries offered many job opportunities. Many Southern Blacks considered it a "promised land." Other cities, such as Philadelphia and New York, were destinations for those moving north.[49]

---

[47] Diffendarfer, J. (2023, November 8). Hobo Code: The Signs and Symbols Used by Travelers of Old. Retrieved from Owlcation.com: https://owlcation.com/humanities/All-things-HOBO-signs-and-symbols.

[48] Gillette, G. (2023, December 25). A Sleeping Giant: Detroit in the Mid-1930s. Retrieved from Sabr.org: https://sabr.org/journal/article/a-sleeping-giant-detroit-in-the-mid-1930s/.

[49] Interactive.com. (2023, December 25). DuSable to Obama. Retrieved from Early Chicago: The Great Migration: https://interactive.wttw.com/dusable-to-obama/the-great-migration.

The migration to the North was not as great as in earlier years and would pick up later during World War II as military production opened up more economic opportunities. Still, the Great Depression was a period where the migration continued and served to change the demographics of many Northern cities. Places such as Detroit did not have sizable African American communities at the turn of the century; this changed dramatically by the end of the Great Depression.

Forced Dislocation

There's a cost-benefit analysis inherent in any public policy decision. This means that no matter how great the benefit to the public a decision or project is, there are costs involved, and some are human costs. The Tennessee Valley Authority (TVA) was a part of the Roosevelt administration's New Deal. Although it generated opportunities and benefits for many Americans, there was a price to be paid for this program, and the residents of Appalachia bore it.

The Tennessee Valley Authority Act became law on May 18th, 1933. The act mandated improvements in the navigability of the Tennessee River, flood control, the economy in the Tennessee Valley, and the operation of the Wilson Dam. It covered a seven-state area, including Alabama, Tennessee, Kentucky, Mississippi, Georgia, Virginia, and North Carolina. Over nine thousand people were employed by the TVA by 1934, and sixteen hydroelectric dams were built between 1933 and 1934. However, the residents of the area also had to pay the piper.

People are shocked at how many homes and villages were flooded by the Three Gorges Dam in China. The same happened in the Tennessee Valley area. Approximately 3,500 families in eastern Tennessee lost their homes when the Norris Dam flooded nearly 239 square miles.[50]

Places that had been populated for generations sank under the water. Loyston, Tennessee, was first inhabited in 1800 and had homes, schools, churches, and business establishments. Willow Grove, Tennessee, had a general store and a grist mill. With over seven hundred families, Butler was the largest town in Tennessee to be flooded. The old Cherokee towns of Chota and Tanasi experienced the same fate.[51]

---

[50] History.com Editors. (2023, June 13). TVA. Retrieved from History.com: https://www.history.com/topics/great-depression/history-of-the-tva.

[51] Watts, J. (2021, May 18). Underwater Ghost Towns of Tennessee. Retrieved from Tnmuseum.org: https://tnmuseum.org/junior-curators/posts/underwater-ghost-towns-of-

The cost was not limited to Tennessee. Waterloo and Riverton, Alabama, were inundated, and over five hundred families were forced to relocate.[52]

To achieve its goals, the TVA exercised its power of eminent domain, a legal principle that allows the government to take private property for public use. This authority permitted the government to legally seize land to construct dams and reservoirs, which would lead to the displacement of residents.

The TVA justified these relocations by arguing that the projects were in the public interest, providing flood control, electricity, and improved agricultural conditions. The goals might have produced important benefits, but they forced the removal of many Appalachian families from their ancestral lands.

The TVA's projects led to the displacement of approximately 125,000 people and the inundation of hundreds of thousands of acres of land. Those displaced families, mostly subsistence farmers living in impoverished conditions, were forced to leave their homes and communities to make way for dams and reservoirs. Although the TVA intended to compensate those affected by its projects, the process was often stymied by various challenges. Families were offered financial compensation for their land and homes, but these payments were often not enough to help rebuild their lives in new locations. The emotional toll of losing ancestral homes and close-knit communities cannot be computed in monetary terms. Those who were relocated faced the difficult task of starting over again.

Life for the average American during the Great Depression was full of economic hardship and general uncertainty. It was a challenging period in American history that had a lasting impact on the economy and social policies in the United States. Change would be essential to allow American society to survive. The transformation of America began on March 4th, 1933, when a man placed his left hand on a Bible and raised his right hand.

---

tennessee.

[52] Tennessee Valley Authority. (2023, December 25). The Lost Towns of Pickwick. Retrieved from Tva.com: https://www.tva.com/About-TVA/Our-History/Built-for-the-People/The-Lost-Towns-of-Pickwick.

Chapter 7: Roosevelt and His New Deal

"We have nothing to fear but fear itself." Those words were spoken on March 4th, 1933, by a man who never saw a hungry day.

Franklin Delano Roosevelt was part of the American aristocracy. He came from a wealthy family and was used to a life of luxury. There was no reason for him to suspect that the wealth or privilege he enjoyed would ever go away. This assurance gave him an appearance of extreme self-confidence. He needed that as he faced a country on its knees.

Things could not have been worse. The banking system was in shambles, people were unemployed, and millions were wandering throughout the nation, hoping to find a decent job or even something to eat. Roosevelt approached these problems with a can-do attitude. The future of American society and democracy depended on the president's ability to deliver on his promises.

Franklin Delano Roosevelt.
https://commons.wikimedia.org/wiki/File:Franklin-roosevelt.JPG

Dark Clouds Everywhere

While Franklin D. Roosevelt projected confidence and optimism during the early days of his administration, it is reasonable to assume that he experienced moments of fear and worry. The Great Depression was an unprecedented crisis, and Roosevelt understood the trials he would face as president.

The severity of the economic crisis would have been a source of concern for any leader. It was the greatest American emergency since the Civil War. Roosevelt's ideas were revolutionary for the time, and he needed to navigate a politically charged environment. Implementing his New Deal policies would require skillful negotiation and persuasion.

Roosevelt's presidency began with high expectations. The public was looking to him for solutions to the economic crisis and expected quick results. On top of all the issues was his personal health. Roosevelt had been diagnosed with polio in 1921, which left him with a disability.

Although he concealed the extent of his disability from the public, it would have been a personal challenge and a source of worry for him.

Roosevelt's leadership style was characterized by an ability to project confidence and provide hope to the American people. He used his communication skills, including his famous fireside chats, to reassure the nation and instill a sense of optimism. Roosevelt's ability to lead the nation through the darkest days played a crucial role in the success of his presidency.

The Bank Holiday

The new president moved quickly. He ordered a bank holiday, which took place shortly after he assumed office on March 4th, 1933. It was a pivotal moment in his efforts to address the Great Depression. The bank holiday was a four-day nationwide closure of all the banks in the United States. It was declared by executive order, and the holiday took place on March 6th, 1933.

The purpose of the bank holiday was to halt the ongoing panic and bank runs threatening the banking system's stability. People were rushing to withdraw their money from banks, further eroding confidence in the financial system. The primary goal of the bank holiday was to restore confidence in the banking system. By temporarily closing the banks, Roosevelt aimed to stop the bank runs and prevent further drain on banks' reserves.

The brief respite allowed regulators and government officials to assess the financial health of individual banks. Those that were solvent and well managed were allowed to reopen, while others were closed or reorganized.

The pause was only part of the overall plan. Congress passed the Emergency Banking Act on March 9th, 1933. This piece of legislation provided the government with increased authority to stabilize and support the financial system, including the ability to provide loans to those in need.[53]

This all may seem like drastic action, but it was necessary. Bank runs would likely have continued and intensified without the brief respite. Desperate people could have taken to the streets in protest or to

---

[53] Federal Reserve History. (2023, December 25). Bank Holiday of 1933. Retrieved from Federalreservehistory.org: https://www.federalreservehistory.org/essays/bank-holiday-of-1933.

demand their money from banks, potentially leading to violence and instability.[54]

Roosevelt's bank holiday was a crucial and timely intervention that halted the immediate crisis in the banking sector, restored public confidence, and set the stage for broader financial reforms. It was a decisive move that helped stabilize the economy.

The First Hundred Days

Franklin D. Roosevelt's first hundred days in office, from March 4th to June 16th, 1933, transformed American history. Roosevelt's presidency ushered in a whirlwind of legislative and executive action. We are going to explore the significance of Roosevelt's first one hundred days, detailing what was accomplished, the impact on American society, the success of these efforts, and the reasons for their importance.

Alphabet Salad

The first hundred days produced a large number of new government agencies tasked with the goal of restoring the American economy. Collectively known as the New Deal, these were groundbreaking initiatives that expanded the scope of the federal government. Several areas of trouble were targeted.

- Banking Reform

  The Emergency Banking Act restored confidence in the nation's banks by declaring a bank holiday and allowing government inspections to identify sound institutions. The Glass-Steagall Act (June 16th, 1933) separated commercial and investment banking, and the Federal Securities Act of 1933 (May 27th, 1933) aimed to regulate the stock market.

- Job Creation

  Roosevelt's administration launched the Civilian Conservation Corps (known as the CCC; it was created on March 31st, 1933) to ease unemployment rates. The Federal Emergency Relief Act (May 12th, 1933) and the National Employment System Act (June 6th, 1933) also helped to provide jobs for the unemployed. These programs put millions of Americans to work on various public works projects.

---

[54] Silber, W. L. (2009, July). Why Did FDR's Bank Holiday Succeed? Retrieved from Newyorkfed.org: https://www.newyorkfed.org/research/epr/09v15n1/0907silb.html.

CCC workers building a culvert.
https://commons.wikimedia.org/wiki/File:Civilian_Conservation_Corps_-_NARA_-_195832.jpg

- Business Reform

  The National Industry Recovery Act (NIRA, created on June 16th, 1933) aimed to address the economic challenges of the Great Depression by regulating and stabilizing industry and labor practices. It created the National Recovery Administration (NRA) to oversee the creation and enforcement of industry codes of fair competition.

- Agricultural Recovery

  The New Deal did not forget the problems faced by farmers and those living in rural areas. The Agricultural Adjustment Act (AAA, created on May 12th, 1933) was followed by the Tennessee Valley Authority (TVA, created on May 18th, 1933) and the Farm Credit Act (created on June 16th, 1933). These acts were all meant to provide badly needed assistance to the agricultural sector of the American economy.[55]

[55] American-historama.org. (2023, December 25). The Hundred Days FDR. Retrieved from American-historama.org: https://www.american-historama.org/1929-1945-depression-ww2-

Immediate Results

Roosevelt's actions were a shot in the arm to an ailing American society. The first hundred days marked a shift in the federal government's role, which assumed a more active and interventionist role in addressing economic and social issues, setting a precedent for future government involvement. The first hundred days were marked by unprecedented legislative and executive action significantly impacting American society. The period also established Franklin Delano Roosevelt as a dynamic and effective leader. His willingness to experiment with bold policies and respond to the needs of the time redefined the presidency. The hundred days remain a testament to the power of courageous leadership and government intervention during times of crisis.

The Second New Deal

The Hundred Days was phase one of Roosevelt's response to the Great Depression. The president initially introduced and signed legislation that gave emergency assistance to an economy and population reeling from bank failures and high unemployment. Phase two would stop those dire conditions from happening again.

The Second New Deal took place from approximately 1935 to 1938 and continued to expand the initiatives introduced during Roosevelt's early years as president. It was characterized by a shift in focus from immediate relief to long-term economic and social reforms. Some of the laws enacted in those years still govern various areas of government policy.

- Social Security Act (August 14th, 1935)

  The Social Security Act established the framework for the modern social safety net in the United States. It provided pensions for retired workers, established unemployment insurance, and gave needed assistance to the disabled and to disadvantaged children.

- Works Progress Administration (WPA; May 6th, 1935)

  WPA employed millions of Americans in a wide range of public works projects, including infrastructure improvements, arts and culture programs, and the construction of public

era/hundred-days.htm.

buildings.

- National Labor Relations Act (Wagner Act; July 5th, 1935)

  The Wagner Act was legislation that protected the rights of workers to engage in collective bargaining and form labor unions. It also created the National Labor Relations Board (NLRB) to enforce labor laws and mediate labor disputes.

- Revenue Act of 1935 (Wealth Tax Act; August 30th, 1935)

  This act increased taxes on high-income earners and corporations, implementing a more progressive tax structure. It aimed to redistribute wealth and generate revenue to fund New Deal programs.

- Rural Electrification Administration (REA; March 20th, 1936)

  The REA aimed to bring electricity to rural areas by providing loans and assistance to rural electric cooperatives. The REA modernized rural America and improved the lives of many rural residents.

- Public Utility Holding Company Act (October 1st, 1935)

  This legislation was passed to regulate the power of large utility holding companies. It guarded consumers from unfair and monopolistic practices in the utilities sector.

- Fair Labor Standards Act (June 25th, 1938)

  While technically passed after the Second New Deal period, this act continued the New Deal's labor reforms. It created child labor restrictions, maximum working hours, a federal minimum wage, and fundamental protections for workers.

The Second New Deal aimed to provide a more comprehensive and lasting solution to economic inequality and social insecurity. The Second New Deal expanded the role of the federal government in regulating the economy, which caused some concern. The United States had not experienced this amount of government regulation before. Roosevelt enjoyed tremendous support for and little opposition to his initial legislative agenda, but he faced criticism for going too far with the Second New Deal.

Many business leaders and corporate interests opposed the Second New Deal's government regulation and expansion of labor protection. They argued that increased government intervention and labor rights infringed on their ability to manage their businesses, which could stifle economic growth. Conservative politicians and interest groups also resisted the expansion of government authority and spending associated with the Second New Deal. They argued that it threatened individual liberty and free-market capitalism. Critics were worried that the president was moving the country closer to socialism.

Liberals, especially the far left, also surprisingly critiqued the Second New Deal. They contended the New Deal was not doing enough to provide relief and assistance to those in need.

The Court Challenges

The United States government has built-in checks and balances to prevent one branch from gaining too much power. Roosevelt and the Democrats controlled the executive and legislative branches. However, the third branch of government, the judicial, was going to frustrate his plans.

The US Supreme Court was a significant obstacle to the Second New Deal. The Supreme Court struck down several key New Deal programs and policies by questioning their constitutionality and arguing the initiatives went beyond the federal government's constitutional authority.

Schechter Poultry Corp. v. United States (1935)

The National Industry Recovery Act and the NRA were the crown jewels of the New Deal. The act had good intentions but poorly written codes (a total of 775 basic and 208 supplementary codes). The president was given the authority to remove unfair trade practices, establish minimum wages and maximum hours, and enforce laborers' rights to bargain collectively. Perhaps the legislation bit off more than it could chew.[56]

The NRA received considerable criticism, and eventually, a court case contesting its constitutionality made its way to the US Supreme Court. On May 27th, 1935, the Supreme Court declared the National Industrial Recovery Act unconstitutional primarily because it found that the law violated the separation of powers by delegating legislative authority to the executive branch. The act exceeded the scope of federal commerce regulation by controlling intrastate activities, lacked specific

[56] Social Welfare History Project. (2023, December 25). The National Recovery Administration (1933-1935). Retrieved from socialwelfare.lbrary.vcu.edu: https://socialwelfare.library.vcu.edu/eras/great-depression/u-s-national-recovery-administration/.

congressional standards, and imposed excessive and overly detailed rules on businesses.

This decision was a major setback for New Deal policies and marked a decisive moment in the Supreme Court's review of the federal government's growth. It was the beginning of the legal problems for the New Deal.

Other Supreme Court decisions hobbled the New Deal. *Humphrey's Executor v. United States* (May 27th, 1935) ruled the president lacked the authority to subjectively remove a federal trade commissioner; it was only possible to do so if the person was inefficient, neglected their duty, or committed malfeasance in office. *United States v. Butler* (January 6th, 1936) declared the 1933 Agricultural Adjustment Act encroached upon the Tenth Amendment by interfering in areas reserved for the states.

The judicial branch was not in step with Roosevelt, and he intended to do something about that.

Court Packing

President Roosevelt proposed to add more justices to the Supreme Court in what was referred to as "court packing." He wanted to reorganize the Supreme Court to force his opponents on the bench to resign and add one new judge for every judge who reached the age of seventy without retiring.

Roosevelt's notion was a disaster. All sides denounced the court-packing scheme, and Roosevelt was accused of trying to be a dictator. The president squandered political capital in pursuing this idea.

The Supreme Court would later rule in favor of New Deal programs, and Roosevelt eventually appointed five justices to the Supreme Court. His image, however, was damaged by the whole affair.[57]

The Roosevelt Recession

The recession of 1937 was a dramatic economic downturn during Franklin D. Roosevelt's second term. It was a sharp contraction of the economy that was unanticipated after several years of recovery and expansion. A leading factor contributing to the recession was a large reduction in federal government spending. To balance the federal budget and address the growing deficit, Roosevelt, along with his

---

[57] Digital History. (2023, December 25). The New Deal in Decline. Retrieved from Digitalhistory.uh.edu: https://www.digitalhistory.uh.edu/disp_textbook.cfm?smtID=2&psid=3450.

economic advisors, decided to scale back government spending and shift toward fiscal conservatism.

The Federal Reserve played a role in this economic downturn. It followed a policy of tightening the money supply, which included increasing bank reserve requirements. These measures attempted to curb inflationary pressures and any speculative excesses in the financial markets. However, they inadvertently harmed the broader economy.

The reduction in government spending and the tightening of monetary policy affected industrial production. Factory output dropped, and businesses began reducing their investments and production levels. As industrial production slowed and unemployment increased, consumer spending also fell. Consumers were cautious amid the economic uncertainty, which contributed to the downturn.

The stock market experienced a sharp decline during this period, erasing gains from the previous years. The economic uncertainty and reduced business activity caused stock prices to go down. Unemployment rates increased, as businesses cut back on hiring and laid off workers in response to the recession.

The recession served to remind policymakers of the economy's weakness and the potential consequences of abrupt fiscal and monetary policy shifts. Roosevelt responded to the recession by increasing government spending and adopting a more accommodating monetary policy, which eventually helped the economy recover.

Economists and historians still debate the effectiveness of the New Deal. Some say not enough was done, and others complain that too much government intervention occurred during the 1930s. It is the stuff of faculty lounge debates. However, some conclusions about the New Deal cannot be dismissed.

Something needed to be done. The economy at the end of 1932 was in a state of disaster. The laissez-faire attitude toward government intervention in the markets was not correcting the situation. Too many Americans were in desperate straits to wait for the market to gradually correct itself. The Great Depression more than likely would have ended with World War II anyway. However, in 1932, that was years in the future. If the government continued to ignore the problems, the human toll would have been enormous.

Franklin Delano Roosevelt can be criticized for some actions, but what he accomplished merits praise. He steered the course, allowing

America to recover while maintaining its institutions. Some may think his actions were extreme. There were other things he could have done that were being utilized in places like Germany and Russia overseas. Those other options were frightening, to say the least.

Chapter 8: International Impact of the Great Depression

The Great Depression was not an isolated economic catastrophe. It rippled across continents, causing extensive consequences for the global economy. The Great Depression had a profound effect on Europe, which was still trying to recover from the calamity of World War I. The Treaty of Versailles imposed heavy war debts and reparations on Germany and other defeated nations, leaving them economically strained. Those nations were not the only states to pay a price for the war. The victors were confronted with war debt repayment as well.

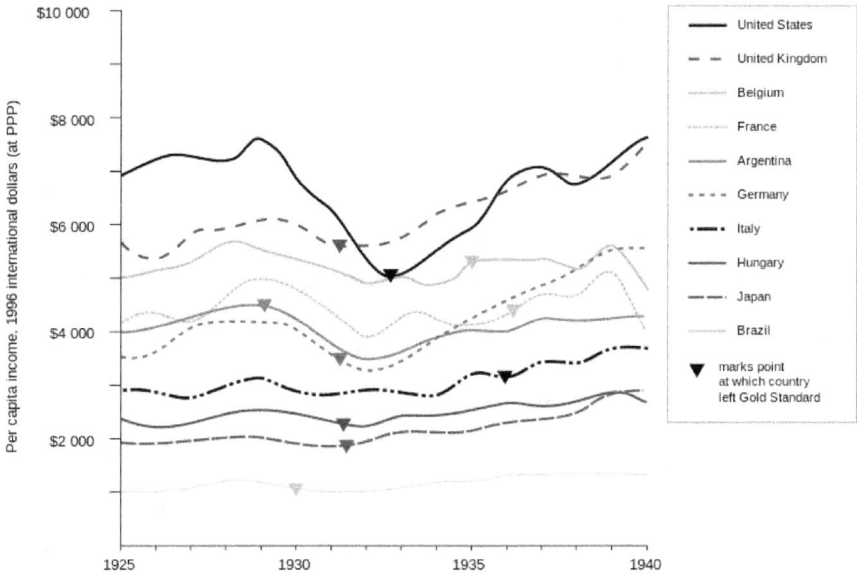

A look at the international impact of the Great Depression.
Will O'Neil (original file)NikNaks talk - gallery - Wikipedia, CC BY-SA 3.0
<https://creativecommons.org/licenses/by-sa/3.0>, via Wikimedia Commons;
*https://commons.wikimedia.org/wiki/File:Graph_charting_income_per_capita_throughout_the_*
Great_Depression.svg

The Debt Burden

The Great War was an expensive victory or defeat, depending on the participant. It had cost greatly to win, and debt weighed heavily on the winners.

Despite being one of the victors, France faced major economic challenges. The country had incurred heavy debts due to the war and was forced to spend a substantial portion of its budget to repay them. The French efforts to get reparation money from Germany were partly meant to help pay off France's war debts. When Germany struggled to make those required payments, France's financial condition worsened, impacting its ability to respond to the economic crisis.

The United Kingdom accumulated sizable debts to finance its military efforts. These debts placed a strain on the British economy, and the government had no choice but to divert scarce resources away from domestic needs to meet its financial obligations. The global economic downturn disrupted international trade, which was a major source of British prosperity. As trade contracted, the UK experienced declining exports and unemployment, making its economic vulnerability worse.

Germany bore the brunt of the penalties of the Treaty of Versailles, which imposed massive reparations payments. The initial reparations figure was set at 132 billion gold marks, an astronomical sum. Germany resorted to printing more money to meet these obligations, leading to hyperinflation. This economic instability damaged the savings of ordinary citizens and undermined confidence in the currency. The financial hardship and instability resulting from war reparations made Germany more susceptible to the shocks of the Great Depression, which only intensified the country's economic woes.[58]

Many Eastern European countries had also incurred debts during the war and had limited capacity to rebuild their economies. The economic difficulties faced by newly formed countries, combined with political instability, made them highly vulnerable to the global financial crisis. Austria, in particular, experienced severe hyperinflation and social unrest.

There was a vicious cycle created by repayment. The United States was the largest creditor and demanded the repayment of loans it gave to the Allies. In turn, the United Kingdom and France pressured Germany to pay the reparations it owed so that those loans could be repaid. Bankers from the United States, in turn, loaned money to Germany so the latter could pay those reparations. Germany eventually defaulted on payments, and France sent troops to occupy the Ruhr.

Abandoning the Gold Standard

The gold standard was no longer a feasible money policy in light of war debts and reparations. When countries abandoned the gold standard in response to the economic crisis of the 1930s, there were various consequences.

- Currency Devaluation

  Many countries abandoned the gold standard to allow their central banks more flexibility to institute monetary policies that would correct economic downturns. As countries left the gold standard, they devalued their currencies to stimulate economic

---

[58] Klein, C. (2023, March 28). How Economic Turmoil After WWI Led to the Great Depression. Retrieved from History.com: https://www.history.com/news/world-war-i-cause-great-depression.

growth and make their exports more competitive. The devaluation made their goods cheaper for foreign buyers, potentially boosting exports.

• Inflation and Deflation

The abandonment of the gold standard contributed to inflation and deflation rates in different countries. Some countries experienced inflation due to currency devaluation, while others faced deflation as prices fell. Inflation and deflation had complex and uneven effects on various sectors of the economy, leading to winners and losers within and between countries.

• Trade Imbalances

Currency devaluations and fluctuations disrupted international trade. Some countries that devalued their currencies gained an advantage in export markets, while others saw their exports become more expensive. Trade imbalances emerged, as countries with strong currencies (typically those still on the gold standard) faced declining export competitiveness while those with weaker currencies benefited.

• Global Economic Instability

The abandonment of the gold standard contributed to economic uncertainty and instability on a global scale. Currency devaluations and fluctuations made it difficult for businesses and investors to predict exchange rates and plan for the future. The uncertainty hindered international investment and trade, aggravating the economic challenges. Countries pursued their own monetary and economic policies without a unified approach. The lack of international cooperation made it harder to effectively address the global economic crisis.

Impact of Leaving Gold Behind

European countries abandoned the gold standard primarily to address the economic turmoil and financial instability. The specific timing and effects of each country's decision to abandon the gold standard varied.

The United Kingdom faced severe economic challenges, including high unemployment and declining industrial production. It abandoned the gold standard on September 21st, 1931, in an effort to devalue the pound and make its exports more competitive. Leaving the gold standard led to the pound being devalued, making British goods more attractive. It boosted British exports, but the decision also contributed to global instability as other countries reacted to the devaluation.[59]

Germany abandoned the gold standard in 1931. The decision was characterized by currency devaluations and fluctuations as Germany grappled with economic challenges.

Countries used currency devaluation and the abandonment of the gold standard as a means to protect their local economy from foreign competition. They went one step further by adopting protectionist policies, including tariffs. These measures made things worse by further reducing international trade and deepening the global economic crisis. These decisions would have repercussions for international trade and financial relations.[60]

European Bank Emergencies

European banks faced a myriad of problems during the Great Depression. European banks were closely interconnected with US banks through loans and investments. As the US banking system faced severe problems, this contagion spread to the European banks, exacerbating their financial difficulties.

The values of many assets held by European banks, such as stocks and real estate portfolios, plummeted because of the economic downturn. This led to sizable losses for financial institutions, eroding their capital positions and solvency. Many European banks held debt issued by governments, companies, and individuals that became increasingly risky as the Great Depression deepened. The inability of debtors to meet their obligations resulted in significant losses for the banks.[61]

---

[59] Brain, J. (2023, December 28). The Great Depression. Retrieved from Historic UK.com: https://www.historic-uk.com/HistoryUK/HistoryofBritain/Great-Depression/.

[60] Mediawiki. (2023, December 28). Abandonment of Gold Standard during Inter-War Period. Retrieved from Mediawiki.midlebury.edu: https://mediawiki.middlebury.edu/IPE/Abandonment_of_Gold_Standard_during_Inter-War_Period.

[61] Wurm, S. (2017, July 2). The Great Depression: Credit-Anstalt Crisis 1931. Retrieved from Central European Economic and Social History.com: http://centraleuropeaneconomicandsocialhistory.com/the-great-depression-credit-anstalt-crisis-1931.

Widespread failures and economic turmoil eroded confidence in the financial system. This lack of trust made it difficult for banks to attract deposits or raise capital to stabilize their positions. Bank failures and economic hardships fueled social unrest and even contributed to the rise of extremist political movements in some cases.[62]

An International Trade War

The Smoot-Hawley Tariff Act was a stick of dynamite that blew up into a sizable trade war. The tariff had a highly damaging impact on international trade. Because the United States was a major global economic player, raising tariffs on a wide array of goods negatively impacted many nations.

The tariff initiated a trade war. Many nations, including Canada, European countries, and trading partners in Latin America, implemented their own protectionist measures and retaliatory tariffs against US exports. This retaliatory trade environment further stifled international trade and economic recovery.[63]

American exporters faced serious problems due to the tariff. As foreign markets became less accessible due to retaliatory tariffs, US exports declined, leading to reduced demand for American goods.

The protectionist policies of the Smoot-Hawley Tariff worsened the overall economic downturn of the Great Depression. The contraction in international trade deepened the global economic crisis. It reduced economic growth, increasing unemployment and economic hardships in many countries. It was seen as a violation of the principle of free trade and international trade agreements, contributing to diplomatic tensions and creating an atmosphere of economic nationalism.[64]

Sinister Alternatives

Capitalism was failing to address Europe's problems during the Great Depression, so alternative solutions began to appear. These solutions

[62] Encyclopedia.com. (2023, December 28). Europe, Great Depression In. Retrieved from Encyclopedia.com: https://www.encyclopedia.com/economics/encyclopedias-almanacs-transcripts-and-maps/europe-great-depression.

[63] Nicole, A. (2023, October 10). The Smoot-Hawley Tarif Act: Economic Protectionism and Its Impact on the Great Depression. Retrieved from Spermoney.com: https://www.supermoney.com/encyclopedia/smoot-hawley-tariff-act.

[64] Britannica.com. (2023, December 28). Smoot-Hawley Tariff Act. Retrieved from Britannica.com: https://www.britannica.com/topic/Smoot-Hawley-Tariff-Act.

offered drastic means of remedying the situation, and although they appeared to provide some help, they were undemocratic and authoritarian. The most prominent movements during this time were communism and fascism.

The Great Depression under Stalin

Although the communist Soviet Union brought untold suffering to many, the nation, under the leadership of Joseph Stalin, paradoxically found itself benefiting from this economic catastrophe. The Soviet Union was relatively isolated from the capitalist nations. While the Western economies plunged into chaos, the Soviet Union's autarkic policies became an asset for its economy. Stalin's government had already embarked on a path of forced industrialization and collectivization in the late 1920s, which aimed at rapidly modernizing the country's infrastructure and agriculture.

The economic downturn in the West provided an opportunity for the Soviet Union to accelerate drastic policies without external interference. The first five-year plan (1928-1932) saw the expansion of heavy industry, particularly in sectors such as steel, coal, and machinery, which laid the foundation for the Soviet Union's industrial might in later decades.

The Soviet Union sought economic cooperation with capitalist nations to secure its survival. The Great Depression provided an incentive for Western countries to engage with the Soviet Union, even if it meant tolerating its communist regime temporarily. Despite the authoritarian nature of Stalin's regime and its blatant disregard for human rights, the United States recognized the Soviet Union diplomatically and formally recognized it as a nation in 1933. Getting closer to the dictatorship was driven by a desire to have access to the Soviet market, particularly for American industrial products.

The agricultural sector in the Soviet Union underwent a tumultuous transformation during the 1930s. The first five-year plan caused terrible consequences. The Holodomor famine in Ukraine killed millions of people and sent whole communities into exile in Siberia and labor camps. While collectivization policies were harshly enforced and created human tragedies on a grand scale, they ultimately allowed the Soviet Union to increase agricultural productivity. Collectivization allowed for the mechanization of agriculture, which boosted grain production and exports, helping the Soviet Union secure foreign exchange.

Stalin's regime skillfully used the Great Depression to promote Soviet communism as a viable alternative to capitalism. The Soviet Union's ability to weather the crisis was portrayed as a triumph of the socialist system, even though the death toll was staggering.[65]

Fascism

The Great Depression helped propel the rise of fascism in Italy and Germany. Economic desperation and political disillusionment pushed many toward extremist ideologies. Benito Mussolini and Adolf Hitler both capitalized on their circumstances through propaganda, charismatic leadership, nationalism, and the repression of the opposition. Both exploited the economic crisis to advance their extremist ideologies and secure power.

- Italy

    Italy was one of the hardest-hit countries during the Great Depression. The existing political system appeared incapable of addressing the issues of high unemployment and economic instability, leading to widespread discontent.

    Benito Mussolini took advantage of this discontent. He promised to restore Italy's greatness through authoritarian rule. He also sought a return to militarism and expansionism.

    The Italian dictator skillfully used propaganda to create an image of himself as Italy's savior. He presented fascism as a dynamic and patriotic alternative to the failing democratic system. The Italian government invested heavily in public works projects to stimulate economic growth and reduce unemployment. These projects included the construction of roads, public buildings, and bridges, giving employment to many Italians who were desperate. Mussolini established the concept of the "corporate state," where different sectors of the economy were organized into corporate entities to promote collaboration between labor and management. The regime tightly controlled labor unions and suppressed strikes to maintain stability and ensure the smooth functioning of the

---

[65] Bennet Sherry, P. (2023, December 28). Global Great Depression. Retrieved from Khan Academy: https://www.khanacademy.org/humanities/whp-1750/xcabef9ed3fc7da7b:unit-7-interwar-and-world-war-ii/xcabef9ed3fc7da7b:7-1-totalitarianism-or-liberal-internationalism/a/read-global-great-depression-beta1.

economy.66

While Italy did experience some economic gains during the Great Depression, these were limited and often very expensive. Mussolini's fascist regime implemented policies aimed at bolstering the Italian economy, but these gains were overshadowed by the regime's authoritarian ambitions.

• Germany

The crippling terms of the Treaty of Versailles after World War I exacerbated Germany's economic woes. Adolf Hitler and the Nazi Party exploited this economic desperation, promising to rebuild the German economy, restore national pride, and eliminate the perceived enemies of the German people.

Hitler and the Nazis promoted an extreme form of nationalism, emphasizing Aryan supremacy and territorial expansion. They spread the idea that communism and the Jewish people were threats to Germany. A combination of electoral success and behind-the-scenes political maneuvering succeeded in Hitler becoming chancellor in 1933.

Germany experienced a complex set of economic developments during the Great Depression, which included both gains and significant challenges. Hitler initiated a series of public works projects, including the construction of highways, stadiums, and public buildings. These projects reduced unemployment. Hjalmar Schacht, appointed as president of the Reichsbank, implemented financial reforms that stabilized the currency and reduced inflation.

Much of Germany's economic recovery resulted from rearmament efforts and military spending. Hitler's government invested heavily in building up the German military, leading to the expansion of the armed forces and the defense industry.[67]

[66] Prativadi, J. (2015, February 17). How Did the Great Depression Affect Italy? Retrieved from Prezi.com: https://prezi.com/pv8viawrr64j/how-did-the-great-depression-affect-italy/.

[67] Facing History.org. (2016, August 2). The Battle for Work. Retrieved from Facinghistory.org: https://www.facinghistory.org/resource-library/battle-work.

The Man Behind the Mask

Communism and fascism gave appearances of economic success and social progress, but it was all an illusion. Gains were made at societal costs that bordered on the horrific. Behind a mask of well-being was evil bordering on madness.

Stalin played a game of masterful deception. He fooled foreign journalists into believing that the Soviet Union was making dramatic progress by using disinformation and propaganda. Foreigners visiting the country were shown carefully scripted examples of progress and denied access to areas of repression. Economic data was deliberately distorted to show a thriving economy that did not exist. The truth was masterfully concealed. The Soviet Union experienced human tragedies and disasters during the Great Depression, many of which were the result of government policies and actions.

The rapid industrialization drive of the first five-year plan led to numerous industrial accidents and unsafe working conditions. Workers faced hazardous environments and a lack of safety regulations. The gulag system of cheap labor provided manpower for industrial projects. Conditions in these camps were notoriously harsh, with forced labor, inadequate food, and poor living conditions being common.

While the Soviet government touted its economic achievements during the Great Depression, rapid industrialization generated economic imbalances and inequalities between urban and rural areas. The first five-year plan disrupted traditional rural life and led to the separation of families. Many individuals were arrested, imprisoned, or executed, leading to the breakdown of families and communities.

Mussolini and Hitler were no better. Mussolini's regime eliminated political opposition, dissolved rival political parties, and established a totalitarian state. His suppression of dissent was ruthless; he used secret police and censorship. The Nazis systematically dismantled democratic institutions, silenced opposition parties, and persecuted minority groups, particularly Jews and political dissidents. The Gestapo and concentration camps played a pivotal role in enforcing Nazi ideology. The oppression was hidden behind deliberate policies of disinformation, and Mussolini and Hitler were made to look like heroes. It is hard to say how much Roosevelt knew about what was going on overseas, but the president was probably informed by his advisors and ambassadors of what the authoritarian regimes in Europe were doing.

The American president was forced to walk a very thin line himself. Roosevelt proposed dramatic changes, but he still had to respect the checks and balances inherent in the American political system. He was no doubt fully aware that mistakes could result in society either swinging to the radical right or the radical left. Fortunately, Roosevelt was able to make significant changes without destroying the American concept of democracy.

Chapter 9: Arts of the Great Depression

The Great Depression contributed significantly to the arts in the United States. Writers, artists, and filmmakers used their respective mediums as means of expression, commentary, and sometimes escape from the harsh realities of life. Various forms of art emerged in the 1930s that enriched American society.

The Gifts of the WPA

The Works Progress Administration (WPA) was lampooned by critics as "We Play Around." The program was dismissed as nothing more than a make-work scheme that did not accomplish much. That is an inaccurate assessment. These New Deal programs not only provided economic relief for artists and cultural workers but also contributed to the preservation and promotion of American culture during a challenging period in history. They left an enduring cultural legacy by supporting the creation of public art, fostering artistic talent, and making the arts more accessible to a broader audience.

Arts Initiatives

The Federal Art Project (FAP), Federal Theatre Project (FTP), Federal Music Project (FMP), and Federal Writers' Project (FWP) were agencies within the WPA that aimed to employ artists, writers, musicians, and theater professionals during the Great Depression. Each of these programs had its own significant achievements and contributions to American culture.

- Federal Art Project (FAP): The FAP was established in 1935. As many as ten thousand artists were employed by the FAP at one time or another. The program created public artworks, murals, posters, and sculptures that enhanced public spaces and celebrated American culture and history. Over 200,000 works were created; some of them are considered the most significant artwork in American history.

  The Coit Tower murals in San Francisco are a notable achievement of the FAP. These murals depict various aspects of Californian life and society during the Great Depression. The Milwaukee Handicraft Project was another success that eventually employed over five thousand unskilled workers.

- Federal Music Project (FMP): The FMP funded performances, music education programs, and the creation of new compositions. The FMP aimed to ensure that music remained accessible to the public during difficult economic times by employing musicians, composers, conductors, and music educators.

  Ultimately, higher standards for musical performance resulted from the FMP's efforts. The project encouraged the creation of new compositions, creating a permanent body of unpublished orchestral works and preserving and advancing American music.[68]

- Federal Theatre Project (FTP): This was another WPA initiative that employed actors, playwrights, and directors to create and perform a wide range of theatrical productions.

  The National Director of the FTP was Hallie Flanagan. She turned the FTP into a federation of regional theaters across the country, allowing millions of Americans to see live theater for the first time.

  The FTP would employ fifteen thousand men and women. It produced various theatrical productions, including classic plays, new works, and experimental theater. An important production was *The Cradle Will Rock* by Marc Blitzstein. Directed by

[68] Encyclopedia.com. (2023, December 28). Federal Music Project (FMP). Retrieved from Encyclopedia.com: https://www.encyclopedia.com/economics/encyclopedias-almanacs-transcripts-and-maps/federal-music-project-fmp.

Orson Welles, this politically charged musical drama highlighted workers' struggles during a labor strike. The FTP's daring and socially relevant productions aimed to engage and educate audiences.

- Federal Writers' Project (FWP): The FWP employed writers, including journalists, historians, and novelists, to document and record American life and culture. Writers produced oral histories and other literary works to preserve the nation's cultural heritage.

The American Guide Series, created by the FWP, included state-specific travel guides. The *New York City Guide* (1939) is a well-known example. These guides provided valuable travel information and captured the unique character and history of various regions of the United States.

Many local cultures were dying as urbane elitists commanded the story of rural and less sophisticated Americans. The FWP turned its attention to the soon-to-be-forgotten, producing the largest body of first-person narratives ever collected. Over 10,000 interviews were recorded.

The most significant oral histories were the conversations with more than two thousand formerly enslaved people. One problem that was encountered was the use of White interviewers. Elderly African Americans might have hesitated to tell the more harrowing stories of slavery, and White interviewers might have wanted to downplay slavery to accommodate the racist notions of the time. However, there were Black writers in "Negro Units" who had discussions with formerly enslaved people in Virginia, Louisiana, and Florida. Despite those challenges, the FWP created the largest archive of enslaved persons' first-person accounts, which are accessible online at the US Library of Congress.[69]

Artistic Achievements

The Great Depression left considerable cultural gifts to the American people; many are considered classics in their respective genres. The bitter realities of everyday life inspired authors, painters, and playwrights

---

[69] Barnett, C. (2022, January 13). The Federal Writers' Project: Exploring "The Greatest Literary Project in History." Retrieved from Bookriot.com: https://bookriot.com/federal-writers-project/.

to express their thoughts about the contemporary human condition.

John Steinbeck is considered one of America's greatest authors. He is celebrated for his powerful and socially relevant novels that captured the struggles of ordinary Americans. His masterpiece, *The Grapes of Wrath* (1939), tells the story of a family's journey westward during the Dust Bowl, providing a moving depiction of migrant workers and poverty. That was not his only Depression-inspired work. Steinbeck's novella, *Of Mice and Men* (1936), follows the lives of two displaced ranch workers, George and Lennie, as they dream of a better life while struggling to survive.

Langston Hughes was a prominent African American poet and writer during the Harlem Renaissance, and his poetry flourished during the Great Depression. His poems often explored the experiences of African Americans and the broader American dream. "Let America Be America Again" (1936) reflects the disillusionment and hope of the era.

Artists flourished thanks to the generosity of the FAP. Grant Wood, creator of the iconic *American Gothic* (1930), was a leading figure in the American Regionalist art movement, and the same can be said of Thomas Hart Benton. Urban realists, such as Isabel Bishop and Reginald Marsh, celebrated urban America.[70]

Murals profoundly impacted American art during the Great Depression. Murals were a powerful medium for social and political commentary, allowing artists to engage broader audiences and address important issues of the time. Diego Rivera, a Mexican artist, played a primary role in shaping the mural movement in the United States. His murals, such as those at the Detroit Institute of Arts, depict industrial and social themes, often focusing on labor and workers' rights.

---

[70] Meyer, I. (2022, February 25). 1930s Art—A Look at the Art and Artists of America after the Fall. Retrieved from Artincontext.org: https://artincontext.org/1930s-art/.

Detroit Industry, North Wall by Diego Rivera.
https://commons.wikimedia.org/wiki/File:Rivera_detroit_industry_north.jpg

The Power of Film

Motion pictures were a means of escape for many Americans, but film was more than fantasy at the Bijou. Motion pictures played a crucial role as an expression of art during the Great Depression, and their importance extended far beyond mere entertainment. Movies were a means of capturing the spirit of the era, offering escapism, commentary, and a reflection of the struggles and aspirations of the American people.

Filmmakers commented on the social and economic issues of the time. Their motion pictures explored themes of unemployment, poverty, inequality, and the human impact of the Great Depression. Films like *The Grapes of Wrath* (1940) portrayed the struggles of Dust Bowl migrants and were a powerful social commentary on poverty and the displacement of people.

Frank Capra was a filmmaker known for socially conscious films. *Mr. Smith Goes to Washington* (1939) is a prime example, addressing political corruption and the power of the individual in a democracy. *Modern Times* (1936), directed by and starring Charlie Chaplin, addressed the dehumanizing effects of industrialization and unemployment. Chaplin's iconic character, the Tramp, symbolizes resilience in the face of adversity.

While many films depicted the struggles of the era, they also often highlighted themes of hope, resilience, and the triumph of the human spirit. These themes resonated with audiences and served as sources of inspiration during difficult times.[71]

Live Theater

Theater productions were based on social reality, and the FTP enabled new theater companies to be founded. African American theater companies, in particular, benefited from government investment.

Many playwrights and performers used the stage to address pressing social issues. One prominent example is *Waiting for Lefty* (1935). This play, written by Clifford Odets, depicted the struggles of New York City taxi drivers and their labor union. It was a powerful call to action for workers' rights and social justice.[72]

Politics and Communism in the Arts

Movie theaters during the Great Depression offered several features, and cartoons were played before and after a full-length movie. One animated short, *Confidence*, gave a brief portrayal of what caused the Great Depression and how to get out of it.[73] Another, *Mr. Nobody for President*, speaks of the frustration Americans felt.[74]

These two cartoons are examples of films being used as commentary. Criticism of the wealthy could be found in Marx Brothers comedies, and subtle endorsements of labor rights could also be found in film.

People in the arts tend to be idealistic, so liberal inclinations are common. During the Great Depression, artists and authors gained inspiration from the social problems ordinary people faced. Thus, their sentiments could lean toward socialism and communism.

Many artists and intellectuals witnessed the suffering of the working class and the poor firsthand, and communism offered a vision of economic equality and the redistribution of wealth that resonated with

---

[71] Cravens, H. (2009). Great Depression: Hollywood Movies and the American Community. Retrieved from Omnilogos.com: https://omnilogos.com/great-depression-hollywood-movies-and-american-community/.

[72] Supersummary.com. (2023, December 28). Waiting for Lefty. Retrieved from Supersummary.com: https://www.supersummary.com/waiting-for-lefty/summary/.

[73] *Confidence*. https://www.youtube.com/watch?v=VjGTCchapOk.

[74] *Mr. Nobody for President*. https://www.youtube.com/watch?v=Z80BrugnLVs.

---

their concerns. The Great Depression was marked by stark social inequalities, racial discrimination, and labor exploitation. Communist ideology promised to address these injustices by establishing a classless society. Communism strongly criticized capitalism, which was blamed for the economic collapse of the Great Depression.

The 1930s was a time of intense intellectual and political debate, and communist ideas were actively discussed and debated. The Soviet Union, under Joseph Stalin's leadership, was seen by some as a bastion of socialist ideals and resistance against fascism. This influenced some artists and intellectuals to align themselves with communism or socialist movements.

During the Great Depression, some artists and writers openly embraced communist ideas and incorporated them into their works. Employment in the WPA allowed them to share their beliefs with the American public. These artists often created works critical of capitalism and promoted social and economic equality.

Many artists and writers were idealistic and believed in the power of ideas to bring about change. Communism provided a utopian vision of a more just and equitable society, which appealed to their sense of idealism and the desire to contribute to a better world. It is essential to understand that while communism did influence creative decisions, many people in the arts were not formal members of the party.[75]

Printmaking also helped spread the message of communism to the general public. Political cartoons published in magazines told stories of social injustice and other sociopolitical subjects.[76]

<u>Champions of the Proletariat</u>

Prominent American artists and writers with communist or socialist sympathies included Langston Hughes, John Steinbeck, Dorothea Lange, and Diego Rivera. Their works reflected the struggles of the working class and people experiencing poverty. These members of the arts community advocated for social change.

---

[75] Britannica.com. (2023, December 28). Political Movements and Social Change. Retrieved from Britannica.com: https://www.britannica.com/money/topic/Great-Depression/Political-movements-and-social-change.

[76] Rudnik, A. (2023, September 18). The Art of the Great Depression. Retrieved from 82nd-and-fifth.metmuseum.org: https://82nd-and-fifth.metmuseum.org/perspectives/articles/2023/9/the-art-of-the-great-depression.

- Langston Hughes

  Langston Hughes was sympathetic to communist ideas, but he was not a member of the Communist Party. He was deeply committed to racial and social justice. Hughes used his poetry and writings to address racial inequality, poverty, and the struggles of the working class. His work often depicted the experiences of African Americans and the injustices they faced, which aligned with many of the Communist Party's ideals. Hughes and other African American writers and artists associated with the Harlem Renaissance saw potential allies in the communist movement, as they shared a commitment to fighting racial discrimination and economic inequality.

  Hughes's association with communism had a noticeable influence on his work. His poetry, in particular, reflected the themes of social and economic struggle, working-class life, and the dreams and aspirations of African Americans. Some of his poems, such as "Good Morning, Revolution," explicitly embraced communist ideals of social change and revolution.

- John Steinbeck

  Like Hughes, John Steinbeck was not a formal member of the party. He was known for his empathy toward the plight of the working class. His novels often portrayed the struggles of ordinary people facing economic hardship, labor exploitation, and social injustice. These themes aligned with the concerns of the Communist Party, which advocated for workers' rights and social equality.

  Throughout his career, Steinbeck wrote extensively on social and economic issues. His

  writings often addressed the inequality and injustice experienced by marginalized and disenfranchised groups. While never explicitly endorsing communism, his work reflected a desire for social reform and a critique of the status quo.

  Steinbeck was associated with individuals and groups sympathetic to leftist and socialist ideas. He had friendships and interactions with fellow writers, artists, and intellectuals who held left-leaning political views.

- Dorothea Lange

Dorothea Lange, the American photographer renowned for her documentary photography, had connections to leftist and progressive circles, including the Communist Party. Her social and political beliefs influenced her work. She was a member of the Photo League, a group of photographers in the United States known for their socially conscious documentary work.

Lange's photography focused on documenting the hardships and struggles of marginalized and impoverished communities, including migrant workers, sharecroppers, and displaced families. Her images vividly portrayed the human toll of economic and social inequalities. Many of her photographs are considered powerful visual critiques of the economic system, which resonated with the concerns of leftist groups.

A strong sense of empathy and humanism characterized Lange's pictures. She believed that photography should serve as a tool for social change and advocated using visual storytelling to raise awareness about social injustice and inequality. Her ability to capture the humanity of her subjects, even in the direst circumstances, made her work highly influential in attracting attention to the struggles of the disenfranchised.

Dorothea Lange's Migrant Mother.
https://commons.wikimedia.org/wiki/File:Lange-MigrantMother02.jpg

- Diego Rivera

  Diego Rivera, the Mexican muralist and painter, was a member of the Mexican Communist Party. He was actively involved in leftist political movements throughout his life. His communist beliefs influenced his art, which he use to promote socialist and revolutionary ideas.

  Many of Rivera's murals depict scenes of social struggle, the history of Mexico, and the exploitation of workers. His art was a form of propaganda for the Mexican Revolution and the international communist movement. He believed that art should serve a social and political purpose, and he used his talent to raise awareness about social injustices and inequalities.

  Rivera's paintings and murals often feature themes related to class struggle, workers' rights, and the plight of the poor and oppressed. He incorporated elements of Soviet art and propaganda into his work, including the use of bold, heroic figures and revolutionary symbols.

Not all artists and intellectuals during the Great Depression were communists or socialists; there was a wide range of political beliefs and artistic styles at the time. However, economic hardships and social inequalities led to a heightened interest in leftist ideologies and political activism within the arts community.

The WPA gradually wound down as America emerged from the Great Depression and World War II began. The program officially ended in 1943, but it left a legacy of government involvement in the arts that continues today.

The arts during the Great Depression served as both a mirror reflecting the harsh realities of the time and a window into the aspirations and resilience of the American people. Through film, painting, sculpture, theater, political cartoons, and poetry, artists made significant contributions to society by offering commentary, solace, and inspiration in one of the darkest periods in American history. Their creative endeavors continue to be a testament to the enduring human spirit in the face of adversity.

Chapter 10: The End and the Legacy

The Great Depression ended due to a combination of factors and events that unfolded over several years. The exact timeline and causes of the end of the Great Depression are the subject of ongoing debate among economists and historians.

The end of the Great Depression was a gradual process, and its exact timing and causes varied by region and economic indicators. While World War II helped end the Great Depression in the United States and other countries involved in the war, it's important to note that not all nations recovered simultaneously. Some regions struggled with economic problems for years after World War II ended.

The New Deal policies implemented by President Franklin D. Roosevelt paved the way for the eventual economic revival. These policies included public works programs, financial regulation, and social safety nets. Although they did not end the Great Depression by themselves, they provided relief and support for millions.

Here are two reasons many historians and economists claim are responsible for ending this saga in history.

- World War II

The outbreak of World War II was a major factor in ending the Great Depression. The war effort led to a massive increase in government spending on military production and infrastructure. This cash surge created jobs and stimulated industrial production, ending the low economic activity and high unemployment rates that characterized the Great Depression.

Despite considerable efforts by the government, unemployment in the United States was at 14.6 percent in 1940. Within a few years, that figure dropped to 1.2 percent, and the gross national product doubled.

World War II was the reason for these dramatic improvements. The United States had become the arsenal for democracy and supplied the Allies with munitions and, eventually, manpower to fight the war. Moreover, the results of the war spurred the economy to progress even further after the guns went silent. Technological advances and productivity gains during the war contributed to economic growth in the post-war period.

These innovations had a long-lasting impact on industries and increased overall economic efficiency. As people found employment and incomes rose, consumers had money to spend. However, the focus on wartime production meant there were fewer consumer goods available, which, in turn, led to pent-up consumer demand once the war ended. A surge in post-war consumer spending further fueled economic growth.[77]

Proponents of the argument that World War II ended the Great Depression argue that the massive increase in government spending led to the end of the Great Depression and post-war prosperity. Critics have an alternative explanation. They argue that it was not the increased government spending but a change in attitude. Before the war, the Roosevelt administration had been in an adversarial relationship with big business, arguing that changes were necessary to end the economic troubles. The anti-business approach to government policy was forced to end when the armed forces needed more munitions to fight the war. Roosevelt relied on big companies like General Motors to provide the tanks to win the fight on the battlefield.

Additionally, the trial-and-error experimentation that characterized the New Deal made a full recovery difficult. The war years produced a consistent foundation that made the United States the dominant

---

[77] Fulmer, R. W. (2009, October 23). World War II Ended the Great Depression. Retrieved from Foundation for Economic Education: https://fee.org/articles/world-war-ii-ended-the-great-depression/.

economic power it became after the war.[78]

Nevertheless, the conditions brought on by World War II significantly contributed to prosperity. People were being paid regularly, and rationing and war-related shortages prohibited their ability to spend freely. Once the war was over, those restrictions were suddenly gone, and consumer demand increased. All that businesses had to do was shift from war production to consumer items.

- The Keynes Effect

Economics was primarily an academic subject before the Great Depression. It became a topic of serious interest when the Roosevelt administration and other policymakers attempted to end the financial crisis. One of the architects of the final recovery was John Maynard Keynes.

Keynesian economics is an economic theory and framework generated by British economist John Maynard Keynes. It emerged during the Great Depression and significantly impacted how governments and policymakers approached financial crises. Keynesian economics proposed a different approach to managing the economy than the classical economic theories that prevailed at the time.

Classical economic theories emphasized that markets would naturally correct themselves. These old ideas were turned upside down by the severity and prolonged nature of the Great Depression.

Keynes argued that recessions and depressions are primarily caused by a deficiency in aggregate demand, which is the total spending in the economy. People and businesses tend to save more and spend less in economic downturns, which leads to a decrease in demand for goods and services.

To combat economic downturns, Keynes advocated for government intervention in the form of fiscal policy. He argued that increased public spending and tax cuts during economic slumps would stimulate the desired aggregate demand.

Keynesian economics stresses the value of counter-cyclical policies. Governments should use fiscal and monetary measures to counteract the

---

[78] Fulmer, R. W. (2009, October 23). World War II Ended the Great Depression. Retrieved from Foundation for Economic Education: https://fee.org/articles/world-war-ii-ended-the-great-depression/.

natural fluctuations in economic activity. During times of economic expansion, policies should try to cool down an overheated economy with increased interest rates and reduced government spending.

Keynesian economics influenced Franklin D. Roosevelt's New Deal policies in the United States. Job creation initiatives, public works programs, and social safety nets were intended to increase demand while providing relief to those who were being harmed by the Great Depression.

The Counter-arguments

While Keynesian economics was predominant during the Great Depression and influenced policy responses, there were competing economic theories and schools of thought that proposed alternative solutions to the economic problems.

Classical economists believed that markets would naturally adjust and restore equilibrium. They advocated for limited government intervention and believed that the economy would eventually self-correct. Economists in the Austrian School, such as Friedrich Hayek, were against government intervention and thought that economic recessions resulted from previous government interventions, such as credit expansion. They advocated for a laissez-faire approach and emphasized the role of market forces.

Keynes argued that the government should have spent more instead of cutting federal spending during the 1937-38 recession to stimulate demand and create jobs. Hayek was a bit more hesitant and believed that government intervention would postpone needed adjustments. To him, government intervention postponed recovery.[79] Hayek would go on to argue in his later work, *The Road to Serfdom*, that the planning created by government programs was a direct threat to private enterprise.[80]

We will let the reader decide which economist was correct. However, it is safe to say that during the Great Depression, Keynes's idea of increased government spending ended considerable human suffering in the United States. Cutting back on government spending later, as Hayek

[79] Dana Galizia, F. P. (2014, June 1). Reconciling Hayek's and Keynes' Views of Recessions. Retrieved from Cepr.org: https://cepr.org/voxeu/columns/reconciling-hayeks-and-keynes-views-recessions.

[80] Hayek, F. v. (2023, December 29). The Abandoned Road. Retrieved from Commanding Heights: https://www.pbs.org/wgbh/commandingheights/shared/minitext/ess_serfdom.html.

proposed, may have prevented the bureaucracies created by the New Deal from becoming even more invasive in American life.

The Great Depression's Effects on Monetary Policy

The Great Depression affected monetary policy, leading to significant changes in how central banks and governments approached monetary management. These changes were driven by the lessons learned from the economic devastation and the need to prevent a similar crisis in the future. Here are some of the critical impacts of the Great Depression on monetary policy:

- Abandoning the gold standard was a revolutionary monetary policy change. The departure from the gold standard allowed central banks to use fiat money and better control their currencies, providing flexibility in monetary policy.

- Before the Great Depression, many central banks, including the Federal Reserve, followed a relatively passive approach to the question of monetary policy. They often allowed the money supply to fluctuate without active intervention. The Great Depression exposed the limitations of this approach, as the money supply contracted sharply, contributing to deflation and economic collapse. The Great Depression demonstrated that policymakers could intervene and lessen a financial emergency by infusing amounts of liquidity into the system, which is what the Sixth District of the Federal Reserve Fed did in 1930 during the bank crisis in Tennessee (Richardson, 2013).

Monetary Policy Significance

Research done years after the Great Depression identified the importance of monetary policies for stabilizing the economy. Milton Friedman's analysis of the Great Depression showed that while there are limitations, the right monetary policy can be an influential force in combating downturns.[81]

Fiscal Reform Resulting from the Great Depression

The economic catastrophe underscored the need for laws to protect the American economy and its consumers from unexpected

---

[81] World History.us. (217, May 27). The Impact of the Great Depression. Retrieved from Worldhistory.us: https://worldhistory.us/american-history/the-impact-of-the-great-depression-on-monetary-policy.php.

consequences. Significant reforms involved the stock market and securities.

The Great Depression prompted the United States government to enact several vital fiscal laws to combat the economic crisis. These New Deal legislative measures authorized programs and policies to provide recovery, relief, and reform during the 1930s. Here are some of the noteworthy laws enacted during and in response to the Great Depression:

- Glass-Steagall Act (1933): A significant reason for the stock market crash in 1929 was banks' involvement in the sale and purchase of securities. The Glass-Steagall Act, also known as the Banking Act of 1933, profoundly influenced the American financial industry. Commercial banking (taking deposits and making loans) was legally separated from investment banking (underwriting and trading securities). The Glass-Steagall Act created the Federal Deposit Insurance Corporation (FDIC) to insure bank deposits and provide greater security for savers.

  Unfortunately, significant provisions of the act that were intended to mitigate possible damage due to investment risks were repealed by the Gramm-Leach-Bliley Act of 1999, leading to the financial crisis of 2007-08.

- Securities Act of 1933: This act was designed to regulate the sale and issuance of securities in the aftermath of the stock market crash of 1929. It required companies to provide investors with comprehensive information about securities being offered for sale.

  Investors were to be protected from any fraudulent activities. The law permitted consumers to file a lawsuit if the underhanded deed harmed them. The prospectus, something that is standard information in today's stock market, was created by this act.[82]

  Securities Exchange Act of 1934: The Securities and Exchange Commission (SEC) was created by this law to regulate and oversee the securities industry, including stock exchanges and

---

[82] Team, C. (2023, December 29). The 1933 Securities Act. Retrieved from Corporate Finance Institute: https://corporatefinanceinstitute.com/resources/equities/1933-securities-act-truth-securities/.

broker-dealers. Its focus was to stop fraud and ensure transparency in financial markets.

The SEC is empowered to order periodic reporting by companies that publicly trade securities. Activities of brokers and dealers were regulated, and inside trader activities were prohibited.

New Deal Protections

Laissez-faire government policies caused human suffering on a grand scale during the Great Depression. The Roosevelt administration introduced legislation to safeguard people from economic disasters and grant specific protections for workers.

A series of laws and reforms were enacted in the United States as part of the New Deal to promote safe working conditions, protect the rights of workers, and create a social safety net for the underprivileged. These statutory measures addressed the economic hardships and vulnerabilities faced by American workers and families.

The Social Security Act, passed in 1935, created a comprehensive social insurance system that provided financial support and a social umbrella to protect various categories of disadvantaged individuals:

- Old-Age Insurance: This program provided financial assistance to retirees, ensuring a basic income for seniors after they stopped working.

- Unemployment Insurance: It established a system of unemployment benefits for workers who lost their jobs involuntarily, offering temporary financial relief.

- Aid to Dependent Children: It provided assistance to single parents and their children, aiming to alleviate poverty among families facing the challenges of single parenthood.

- Aid to the Blind and Disabled: Financial support was given to those who were blind or disabled and unable to work.

The overall intent of the Social Security Act was to empower the government to better protect those who were placed in harm's way through no fault of their own. Public policy would no longer insist that self-reliance was the only solution for the disadvantaged.

Various state and federal agencies began implementing regulations and safety standards aimed at promoting safe working conditions and protecting workers from workplace hazards. While many of these regulations were developed later, the groundwork for occupational safety and health laws began during the New Deal era.

The Fair Labor Standards Act (FLSA) was enacted in 1938 to establish several essential standards for working conditions:

- Minimum Wage: The law established a federal minimum wage, ensuring workers received a fair wage for their labor.

- Maximum Working Hours: It introduced maximum working hour standards, limiting the workweek to forty hours for covered employees and providing overtime pay for hours worked beyond that limit.

- Child Labor Provisions: The FLSA included restrictions on child labor, setting age and hour limitations to protect young workers from exploitation.

The National Labor Relations Act (commonly known as the Wagner Act) is a foundation stone for American labor relations. The Wagner Act, which was passed in 1935, was a pivotal piece of legislation that protected workers' rights to organize and bargain collectively:

- Union Rights: It protected the rights of employees to join labor organizations and engage in collective bargaining with management. Its passage resulted in increased efforts to unionize and enable collective bargaining.

- Prohibition of Unfair Labor Practices: This law stopped employers from engaging in unfair labor practices that hindered workers' rights to unionize and bargain collectively.

These laws and initiatives were a significant shift in government policy. They continue to shape labor and social policy in the United States and contribute to a more equitable and secure society.

In Summary

The Great Depression ended through a combination of factors that included the economic stimulus of World War II, increased government spending that created employment, a surge in consumer demand, and changes in monetary policies.

The New Deal profoundly influenced American society, and it is the enduring legacy of the Roosevelt administration. It was instrumental in helping the United States recover from the depths of the Great Depression. The public works programs, job creation initiatives, and financial regulations provided much-needed relief and stimulated economic activity, reducing unemployment and stabilizing the banking system.

The New Deal represented a momentous expansion of the federal government's role in the economy. It marked a departure from laissez-faire economic policies and signaled the government's willingness to intervene actively in economic affairs to address crises and promote the welfare of citizens. This interventionist approach set the stage for developing the modern welfare state. Many of the New Deal's essential programs and principles inspire American governance and social policy today.

Conclusion

The United States survived the Great Depression and became one of the greatest economic powers in world history. America's superpower status does not mean we have forgotten that desperate period in the 1930s. In fact, it is impossible to ignore it because reminders surround us. It is more than just libraries and museums built under the WPA. There are substantial parts of our economy and culture that we take for granted that have their roots in the Great Depression.

Safeguards are there to prevent the stock market from suddenly crashing into chaos. These have permitted us to survive economic episodes that would have destroyed the United States if certain protections were not in place. The stock market is much more sophisticated than it was ninety years ago. The rules and regulations of the SEC and other government guidelines ensure greater safety for investors, a kind of assurance that was unknown in 1929.

The days of government being a casual bystander in people's lives were over. The American public wanted certain protections and believed that government should play a role in their lives. Social Security and other social welfare programs, unheard of before the Great Depression, are now integral parts of many people's lives.

Broadcast media became an essential part of life. Roosevelt used his fireside chats to explain the various programs he was trying to institute. Radio was a very effective communicator of ideas and opinions.

Arts and culture progressed dramatically during the New Deal. Many people could see live theater, and visual arts reached high levels of sophistication. The movies became a centerpiece of American culture and continue to be a powerful force in American art.

The ordinary people who endured the harsh times of the early days had faith in the programs that were part of the New Deal and stuck to it through thick and thin. What is interesting is that Americans kept their institutions and their freedoms. Other countries suffered violent disturbances and authoritarian regimes. Americans did not have that happen to them. The government was allowed a role in their lives, but that didn't mean mass arrests and purges.

There is no question that the Great Depression shaped the character of the young people who experienced it. They grew up to be America's greatest generation. Many were the first members of their families to attend college, and millions went to war after the bombing of Pearl Harbor. Those who soldiered on through the harsh days of the Great Depression were the same ones who, a few years later, were storming the beaches at Normandy, fighting to end fascism and authoritarian regimes.

The Great Depression was a great test for Americans. History shows they passed with flying colors.

If you enjoyed this book, a review on Amazon would be greatly appreciated because it would mean a lot to hear from you.

To leave a review:
1. Open your camera app.
2. Point your mobile device at the QR code.
3. The review page will appear in your web browser.

Thanks for your support!

Here's another book by Enthralling History that you might like

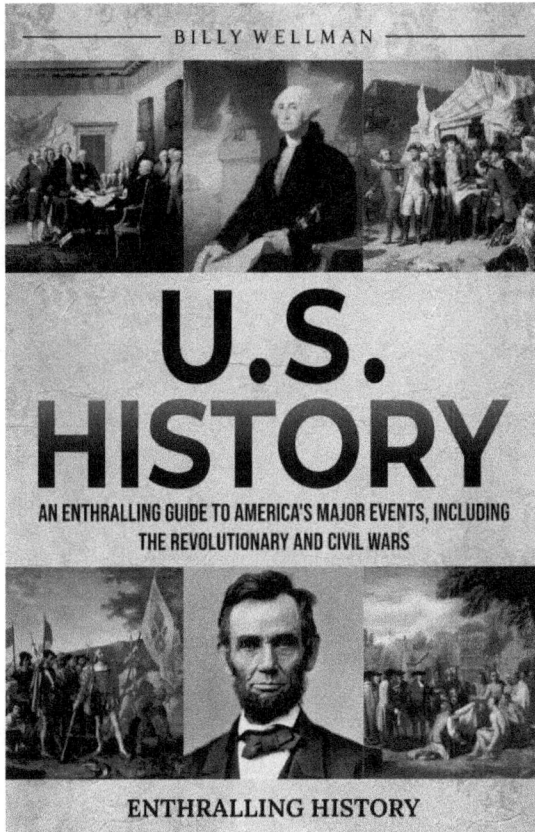

BILLY WELLMAN

U.S. HISTORY

AN ENTHRALLING GUIDE TO AMERICA'S MAJOR EVENTS, INCLUDING THE REVOLUTIONARY AND CIVIL WARS

ENTHRALLING HISTORY

Free limited time bonus

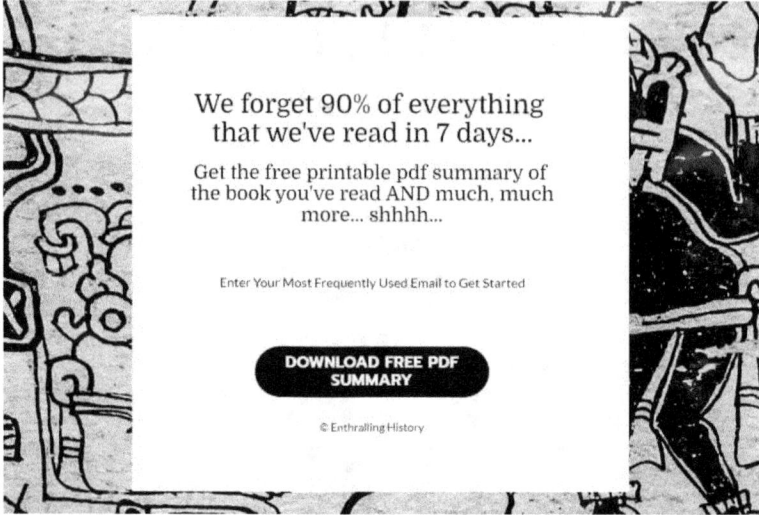

We forget 90% of everything
that we've read in 7 days...

Get the free printable pdf summary of
the book you've read AND much, much
more... shhhh...

Enter Your Most Frequently Used Email to Get Started

**DOWNLOAD FREE PDF
SUMMARY**

© Enthralling History

Stop for a moment. We have a free bonus set up for you. The problem is this: we forget 90% of everything that we read after 7 days. Crazy fact, right? Here's the solution: we've created a printable, 1-page pdf summary for this book that you're reading now. All you have to do to get your free pdf summary is to go to the following website: **https://livetolearn.lpages.co/enthrallinghistory/**

Or, Scan the QR code!

Once you do, it will be intuitive. Enjoy, and thank you!

Bibliography

Amadeo, K. (2021, January 27). Black Thursday 1929, What Happened, and What Caused It. Retrieved from The balance: https://www.thebalancemoney.com/black-thursday-1929-what-happened-and-what-caused-it-3305817.

Amadeo, K. (2021, March 4). Black Tuesday, Its Causes and How It Kicked Off the Depression. Retrieved from The balance: https://www.thebalancemoney.com/black-tuesday-definition-cause-kickoff-to-depression-3305819.

Amadeo, K. (2022, March 28). 1920s Economy. Retrieved from The balancemoney.com: https://www.thebalancemoney.com/roaring-twenties-4060511.

American-historama.org. (2023, December 25). The Hundred Days FDR. Retrieved from American-historama.org: https://www.american-historama.org/1929-1945-depression-ww2-era/hundred-days.htm.

Angola Transparency. (2023, December 23). What Role Did Credit Play in the 1920s. Retrieved from Angolatrasparemcy.blog: https://angolatransparency.blog/en/what-role-did-credit-play-in-the-1920s/.

Au, T. (2015, January 21). Was the Stock Market Crash of 1929 a Cause or Result of the Great Depression? Retrieved from History.stackexchange.com: https://history.stackexchange.com/questions/19038/was-the-stock-market-crash-of-1929-a-cause-or-result-of-the-great-de.

Barnett, C. (2022, January 13). The Federal Writers' Project: Exploring "The Greatest Literary Project in History." Retrieved from Bookriot.com: https://bookriot.com/federal-writers-project/.

Bennet Sherry, P. (2023, December 28). Global Great Depression. Retrieved from Khan Academy: https://www.khanacademy.org/humanities/whp-1750/xcabef9ed3fc7da7b:unit-7-interwar-and-world-war-ii/xcabef9ed3fc7da7b:7-1-totalitarianism-or-liberal-internationalism/a/read-global-great-depression-beta1.

Brain, J. (2023, December 28). The Great Depression. Retrieved from Historic UK.com: https://www.historic-uk.com/HistoryUK/HistoryofBritain/Great-Depression/.

Britannica.com. (2023, November 26). Holodomor. Retrieved from Britannica.com: https://www.britannica.com/event/Holodomor

Britannica.com. (2023, December 28). Political Movements and Social Change. Retrieved from Britannica.com: https://www.britannica.com/money/topic/Great-Depression/Political-movements-and-social-change.

Britannica.com. (2023, December 28). Smoot-Hawley Tariff Act. Retrieved from Britannica.com: https://www.britannica.com/topic/Smoot-Hawley-Tariff-Act.

Cameron, L. A. (2022, June 30). Agricultural Depression 1920-1924. Retrieved from Mnopedia.org: https://www.mnopedia.org/agricultural-depression-1920-1934.

Cassidy, D. (2022, August 6). Weather Wonders: The Dust Bowl. Retrieved from KWWL.com: https://www.kwwl.com/weather/blog/weather-wonders-the-dust-bowl/article_5ad85530-079c-11ed-9e6d-77fc5127444e.html.

Colombo, J. (2012, June 26). The 1920s Florida Real Estate Bubble. Retrieved from hebubblebubble.com: https://www.thebubblebubble.com/florida-property-bubble/.

Cravens, H. (2009). Great Depression: Hollywood Movies and the American Community. Retrieved from Omnilogos.com: https://omnilogos.com/great-depression-hollywood-movies-and-american-community/.

Dana Galizia, F. P. (2014, June 1). Reconciling Hayek's and Keynes' Views of Recessions. Retrieved from Cepr.org: https://cepr.org/voxeu/columns/reconciling-hayeks-and-keynes-views-recessions.

Deceptology. (2022, November 29). The Prosperity of the 1920s: An Illusion for Many. Retrieved from Deceptology.com: https://www.deceptology.com/deceptive/the-prosperity-of-the-1920s-an-illusion-for-many.html.

Diffendarfer, J. (2023, November 8). Hobo Code: The Signs and Symbols Used by Travelers of Old. Retrieved from Owlcation.com: https://owlcation.com/humanities/All-things-HOBO-signs-and-symbols.

Digital History. (2023, December 24). President Hoover. Retrieved from Digital History.uh.edu: https://www.digitalhistory.uh.edu/disp_textbook.cfm?smtID=2&psid=3436.

Digital History. (2023, December 25). The New Deal in Decline. Retrieved from Digitalhistory.uh.edu: https://www.digitalhistory.uh.edu/disp_textbook.cfm?smtID=2&psid=3450.

Editors, H. (2023, April 24). Dust Bowl. Retrieved from History.com: https://www.history.com/topics/great-depression/dust-bowl.

Encyclopedia.com. (2023, December 25). Education 1929-1941. Retrieved from Encyclopedia.com: https://www.encyclopedia.com/education/news-and-education-magazines/education-1929-1941.

Encyclopedia.com. (2023, December 28). Europe, Great Depression In. Retrieved from Encyclopedia.com: https://www.encyclopedia.com/economics/encyclopedias-almanacs-transcripts-and-maps/europe-great-depression.

Encyclopedia.com. (2023, December 28). Federal Music Project (FMP). Retrieved from Encyclopedia.com: https://www.encyclopedia.com/economics/encyclopedias-almanacs-transcripts-and-maps/federal-music-project-fmp.

Encyclopedia.com. (2023, December 25). Public Health 1929-1941. Retrieved from Encyclopedia.com: https://www.encyclopedia.com/education/news-and-education-magazines/public-health-1929-1941.

Encyclopedia.com. (2023, December 24). Farm Foreclosures. Retrieved from Encyclopedia.com: https://www.encyclopedia.com/economics/encyclopedias-almanacs-transcripts-and-maps/farm-foreclosures.

Encyclopedia.com. (2023, December 24). Farm Relief 1929-1941. Retrieved from Encyclopedia.com: https://www.encyclopedia.com/education/news-and-education-magazines/farm-relief-1929-1941.

Encyclopedia.com. (2023, December 24). Great Depression in the South. Retrieved from Encylopedia.com: https://www.encyclopedia.com/economics/encyclopedias-almanacs-transcripts-and-maps/south-great-depression.

Facing History.org. (2016, August 2). The Battle for Work. Retrieved from Facinghistory.org: https://www.facinghistory.org/resource-library/battle-work.

Federal Reserve History. (2023, December 25). Bank Holiday of 1933. Retrieved from Federalreservehistory.org: https://www.federalreservehistory.org/essays/bank-holiday-of-1933.

Firey, T. A. (2014, September 23). How Government Caused the Great Depression. Retrieved from The Maryland Public Policy Institute:

https://www.mdpolicy.org/research/detail/how-government-caused-the-great-depression.

Florida State College at Jacksonville. (2023, December 23). The Great Depression and President Hoover's Response. Retrieved from fscj.pressbooks.pub: https://fscj.pressbooks.pub/modernushistory/chapter/brother-can-you-spare-a-dime-the-great-depression/.

Fulmer, R. W. (2009, October 23). World War II Ended the Great Depression. Retrieved from Foundation for Economic Education: https://fee.org/articles/world-war-ii-ended-the-great-depression/.

Gary Richardson, A. K. (2023, December 23). Stock Market Crash of 1929. Retrieved from Federal Reserve History: https://www.federalreservehistory.org/essays/stock-market-crash-of-1929.

Gilderlehrman.org. (2023, December 23). Herbert Hoover's Inaugural Address, 1929. Retrieved from Gilderlehrman.org: https://www.gilderlehrman.org/history-resources/spotlight-primary-source/herbert-hoovers-inaugural-address-1929.

Gillette, G. (2023, December 25). A Sleeping Giant: Detroit in the Mid-1930s. Retrieved from Sabr.org: https://sabr.org/journal/article/a-sleeping-giant-detroit-in-the-mid-1930s/.

Hayek, F. v. (2023, December 29). The Abandoned Road. Retrieved from Commanding Heights: https://www.pbs.org/wgbh/commandingheights/shared/minitext/ess_serfdom.html.

Herbert Hoover Presidential Library and Museum. (2023, December 24). The Great Depression. Retrieved from Hoover.archives.gov: https://hoover.archives.gov/exhibits/great-depression.

History.com. (2023, November 16). Stock Market Crash of 1929. Retrieved from History.com: https://www.history.com/topics/great-depression/1929-stock-market-crash.

History.com Editors. (2022, March 29). Herber Hoover. Retrieved from History.com: https://www.history.com/topics/us-presidents/herbert-hoover.

History.com Editors. (2023, June 13). TVA. Retrieved from History.com: https://www.history.com/topics/great-depression/history-of-the-tva.

Interactive.com. (2023, December 25). DuSable to Obama. Retrieved from Early Chicago: The Great Migration: https://interactive.wttw.com/dusable-to-obama/the-great-migration.

Kenton, W. (2023, March 16). Stock Market Crash of 1929: Definition, Causes, Effects. Retrieved from Investopedia.com: https://www.investopedia.com/terms/s/stock-market-crash-1929.asp.

Klein, C. (2023, September 26). Before FDR, Herbert Hoover Tred His Own "New Deal." Retrieved from History.com: https://www.history.com/news/great-depression-herbert-hoover-new-deal.

Klein, C. (2023, March 28). How Economic Turmoil After WWI Led to the Great Depression. Retrieved from History.com: https://www.history.com/news/world-war-i-cause-great-depression.

Konkel, L. (2023, January 20). Life for the Average Family during the Great Depression. Retrieved from History.com: https://www.history.com/news/life-for-the-average-family-during-the-great-depression.

Longley, R. (2020, May 26). Hoovervilles: Homeless Camps of the Great Depression. Retrieved from ThoughtCo.com: https://www.thoughtco.com/hoovervilles-homeless-camps-of-the-great-depression-4845996.

McGee, S. (2021, May 13). How Bank Failures Contributed to the Great Depression. Retrieved from History.com: https://www.history.com/news/bank-failures-great-depression-1929-crash.

Mediawiki. (2023, December 28). Abandonment of Gold Standard during Inter-War Period. Retrieved from Mediawiki.midlebury.edu: https://mediawiki.middlebury.edu/IPE/Abandonment_of_Gold_Standard_during_Inter-War_Period.

Meyer, I. (2022, February 25). 1930s Art—A Look at the Art and Artists of America after the Fall. Retrieved from Artincontext.org: https://artincontext.org/1930s-art/.

National Park Service. (2023, December 24). The Emergence of the Great Humanitarian. Retrieved from NPS.gov: https://www.nps.gov/articles/emergence-of-the-great-humanitarian.htm.

National Security Agency/Central Security Service. (2021, August 4). Hobo Communications: A Brief History of Hobos and Their Signs. Retrieved from Nsa.gov: https://www.nsa.gov/History/National-Cryptologic-Museum/Exhibits-Artifacts/Exhibit-View/Article/2718897/hobo-communications-a-brief-history-of-hobos-and-their-signs/

Nicole, A. (2023, October 10). The Smoot-Hawley Tarif Act: Economic Protectionism and Its Impact on the Great Depression. Retrieved from Spermoney.com: https://www.supermoney.com/encyclopedia/smoot-hawley-tariff-act.

Pettinger, T. (2020, April 1). Unemployment during the Great Depression. Retrieved from Economic help: https://www.economicshelp.org/blog/162985/economics/unemployment-during-the-great-depression/.

Prativadi, J. (2015, February 17). How Did the Great Depression Affect Italy? Retrieved from Prezi.com: https://prezi.com/pv8yiawrr64j/how-did-the-great-depression-affect-italy/.

Richardson, G. (2013, September). Banking Crisis and the Federal Reserve as a Lender of Last Resort during the Great Depression? Retrieved from National Bureau of Economic Research: https://www.nber.org/reporter/2013number3/banking-crises-and-federal-reserve-lender-last-resort-during-great-depression.

Richardson, G. (2023, December 24). Banking Panics of 1930-31. Retrieved from Federal Reserve History: https://www.federalreservehistory.org/essays/banking-panics-1930-31.

Roos, D. (2023, March 27). Here Are Warning Signs Investors Missed before the 1929 Crash. Retrieved from History.com: https://www.history.com/news/1929-stock-market-crash-warning-signs.

Rudnik, A. (2023, September 18). The Art of the Great Depression. Retrieved from 82nd-and-fifth.metmuseum.org: https://82nd-and-fifth.metmuseum.org/perspectives/articles/2023/9/the-art-of-the-great-depression.

Science.Smith. (2023, December 24). The Dust Bowl (c.1930-1940). Retrieved from Science.Smith.edu: https://www.science.smith.edu/climatelit/the-dust-bowl/.

Silber, W. L. (2009, July). Why Did FDR's Bank Holiday Succeed? Retrieved from Newyorkfed.org: https://www.newyorkfed.org/research/epr/09v15n1/0907silb.html.

Social Welfare History Project. (2023, December 25). The National Recovery Administration (1933-1935). Retrieved from socialwelfare.lbrary.vcu.edu: https://socialwelfare.library.vcu.edu/eras/great-depression/u-s-national-recovery-administration/.

Supersummary.com. (2023, December 28). Waiting for Lefty. Retrieved from Supersummary.com: https://www.supersummary.com/waiting-for-lefty/summary/.

Team, C. (2023, December 24). Smoot-Hawley Tariff Act. Retrieved from Corporatefinancenstitute.com: https://corporatefinanceinstitute.com/resources/economics/smoot-hawley-tariff-act/.

Team, C. (2023, December 29). The 1933 Securities Act. Retrieved from Corporate Finance Institute: https://corporatefinanceinstitute.com/resources/equities/1933-securities-act-truth-securities/.

Tennessee Valley Authority. (2023, December 25). The Lost Towns of Pickwick. Retrieved from Tva.com: https://www.tva.com/About-TVA/Our-History/Built-for-the-People/The-Lost-Towns-of-Pickwick.

Theodore Phalan, D. Y. (2012, February 29). The Smoot-Hawley Tariff and the Great Depression. Retrieved from Fee.org: https://fee.org/articles/the-smoot-hawley-tariff-and-the-great-depression/.

U-S-history.com. (2023, December 24). Hoover's Early Relief Efforts. Retrieved from U-S-history.com: https://www.u-s-history.com/pages/h1533.html.

Watts, J. (2021, May 18). Underwater Ghost Towns of Tennessee. Retrieved from Tnmuseum.org: https://tnmuseum.org/junior-curators/posts/underwater-ghost-towns-of-tennessee.

Wilhite, D. A. (2023, December 24). The Encyclopedia of Oklahoma History and Culture: Dust Bowl. Retrieved from Oklahoma Historical Society: https://www.okhistory.org/publications/enc/entry.php?entry=DU011#:~:text=As%20a%20result%2C%20dust%20storms,Colorado%20and%20northeastern%20New%20Mexico.

World History.us. (217, May 27). The Impact of the Great Depression. Retrieved from Worldhistory.us: https://worldhistory.us/american-history/the-impact-of-the-great-depression-on-monetary-policy.php.

Wurm, S. (2017, July 2). The Great Depression: Credit-Anstalt Crisis 1931. Retrieved from Central European Economic and Social History.com: http://centraleuropeaneconomicandsocialhistory.com/the-great-depression-credit-anstalt-crisis-1931.

Yeats, W. B. (2923, December 23). The Second Coming. Retrieved from Poetry Foundation.org: https://www.poetryfoundation.org/poems/43290/the-second-coming.

www.ingramcontent.com/pod-product-compliance
Lightning Source LLC
La Vergne TN
LVHW051747080426
835511LV00018B/3257